Christmas
papercrafts

Christmas
papercrafts
Corinne Bradd

David and Charles

www.rucraft.co.uk

ISBN-13: 978-0-7153-2988-7 hardback
ISBN-10: 0-7153-2988-X hardback
ISBN-13: 978-0-7153-2994-8 paperback
ISBN-10: 0-7153-2994-4 paperback

Printed in China by R R Donnelley
for David & Charles
Brunel House   Newton Abbot   Devon

Commissioning Editor: Jennifer Fox-Proverbs
Editor: Bethany Dymond
Assistant Editor: Kate Nicholson
Project Editor: Cheryl Brown
Art Editor: Sarah Clark
Designers: Sarah Underhill, Sabine Eulau and Mia Farrant
Production Controller: Beverley Richardson
Photographers: Karl Adamson and Ginette Chapman

Visit our website at www.davidandcharles.co.uk

David & Charles books are available from all good bookshops;
alternatively you can contact our Orderline on 0870 9908222 or
write to us at FREEPOST EX2 110, D&C Direct, Newton Abbot,
TQ12 4ZZ (no stamp required UK only); US customers call
800-289-0963 and Canadian customers call 800-840-5220.

Contents

Introduction

Everyone enjoys receiving a handcrafted card at Christmas. With so many designs to choose from, your family and friends are sure to be surprised by these special greetings.

I love Christmas and the preparations leading up to it, particularly making handmade cards and decorations from paper, and there is no doubt that I have my mother to thank for this. In my childhood we would spend hours together at the dining-room table making all sorts of wonderful things. Out came my mother's stash of gold card, sticky-backed paper, crêpe paper and thick-cut glitter, and we got to work making crackers, paper chains and lanterns, and tree decorations. We decorated candles with pinned sequins and fake greenery, we cut snowflakes from white paper to stick to every window, and we made stacks of hand-drawn cards. My father still has some of my early efforts tucked away in the loft, and when I see them I remember happy hours spent by my mother's side.

I have made a career from my early love of papercrafts, and a great deal of my professional time is spent designing projects for crafting magazines. Due to magazine production requirements, I will be working on the Christmas issues during the long, hot months of summer. By designing Christmas projects during sun-filled days, I am inspired to experiment with different colour combinations, materials and motifs, and my designs bring a contemporary spin to traditional classics.

I always make time at Christmas to create handcrafted decorations with my daughter just like my mother did with me. Many of the projects in this book are great to make with children or grandchildren so you too can share the simple pleasures of papercrafting with them. I hope that by doing so you will pass on the lesson I learnt crafting alongside my mother; that Christmas is not about how much money is spent on us, but how much time we have spent enjoying it together.

ABOUT THIS BOOK

If you are a keen papercrafter you are likely to have most of the tools and equipment needed to get started straight away. As for materials, I have no doubt that most of you will have paper stashes that can easily be adapted for the projects shown. But don't let that stop you from taking the chance to buy the season's latest offerings.

For those new to papercrafting, the Basic Tool Kit (pages 10–11), Christmas Papers (pages 12–13) and Christmas Embellishments (pages 14–17) features will ensure you are tooled up with the right equipment and materials before you begin work on the projects you choose to make.

To help you make your project selection, I have organized the designs into three sections: Greetings is packed with ideas for making handcrafted tags and cards; Giving has simple present and presentation projects; and Decorating features papercrafted accents to brighten up your home during the festivities. Each section opens with photographs of the main designs included, but many of the chapters have an added bonus project giving alternative ways to adapt the main ideas so do look out for these.

You Will Need lists are detailed for each main and alternative project, although I do encourage you to take a flexible approach to these and adapt them to materials you may have an abundance of. If you want to replicate the projects exactly, full details of Suppliers are given at the back of the book on page 127. All the projects are outlined in step-by-step detail, and the Basic Techniques section, pages 18–21, will give extra support and advice for core techniques used, together with guidance on decorating and making envelopes. All the Templates required for the projects can be found on pages 118–126.

In Greetings, the Tags Galore chapter shows how, by building up layers of decoration, you can really lift your projects to make them something special. Matting (placing one layer on top of another so that the bottom layer is just visible) is a technique I like to use often.

In **Giving**, the Star Gift Bag illustrates how the papers you choose can be further embellished to ensure that your designs are unique. Here a stamped snowflake motif is enhanced by heat embossing for a raised effect.

In **Decorating**, the Sleigh Sweet Dish is an example of a simple project made sensational. It is made from just two types of card. I loved designing the decorative glitter card side panels and the stunning end result made the intricate cutting of the design worthwhile.

BASIC TOOL KIT

Before you begin to make your Christmas papercraft projects it is worth gathering together a basic tool kit of items that you are likely to need time and time again. The project instructions assume that you have the following items, but specific equipment and material requirements are listed in the project You Will Need listing, and many of these specific requirements are previewed in Christmas Papers (pages 12–13) and Christmas Embellishments (pages 14–17).

Tracing paper, a pencil and eraser are needed for tracing and transferring templates. Lightweight white card is perfect for making templates for re-using. When working with a pencil, use an HB pencil for drawing templates and cutting lines, and a 2B pencil for marks that will be erased later. Always use a good, soft plastic eraser that does not smudge and keep a sharpener handy to make sure your pencil point is always sharp. A plastic ruler is fine for measuring, and a compass will enable you to draw semicircles and circles of specific diameters.

General-purpose craft scissors are ideal for cutting and trimming paper and card, but for cutting more intricate work you will also need a pair of small, pointed scissors.

When cutting long straight lines, use a craft knife against a metal ruler (never be tempted to use a plastic ruler as the knife can cut nicks in it, making it unusable). Replace the craft knife blades regularly, as a blunt blade will not leave a clean cut. A rotating craft knife may be useful for cutting intricate designs: it has

Although not essential, rotary cutters or paper trimmers take the hard work out of cutting card and paper.

a small, detachable blade that swivels 360° for precision cutting. Always use a **self-healing cutting mat** as it is smooth, flat and easier to cut on than other surfaces, and it will also protect your work surface. Most mats are marked with measuring gauges, which will prove useful when cutting long strips of paper for example.

Keep a range of different types of **glues** and **adhesives** to hand. **Glue sticks**, tubes of solid glue that can be rubbed over areas to leave a sticky residue, are ideal for gluing paper to paper. For a stronger bond, for sticking gemstones or buttons for example, use **PVA glue**, strong all-purpose glue that becomes transparent when dry.

Double-sided tape is quick and clean to use and is invaluable for adding layers to a design, and **3D foam pads** are great for attaching paper shapes and raising them from the surface.

Other tools that are likely to prove useful are a **bone folder** for neatly creasing and folding card, scoring paper and smoothing creases; a **pricking tool** for pricking small holes in paper before stitching; a **fine brush** for brushing away glitter; and a **hole punch** for punching holes in paper and card. A **single hole punch** is useful for cutting small holes when positioning brads and for making holes in tags.

CHRISTMAS PAPERS

Let your imagination run wild when selecting cards and papers for your Christmas projects. Textures, patterns, colours – all can inspire you to bring a new spin to traditional Christmas motifs.

PAPER AND CARD

Paper and card are vital ingredients in papercrafting, and there is a wide variety to choose from, including plain, pearlescent, mirror, patterned, holographic, and many more. Go for the best quality you can find. Paper is sold in A4 (US letter) sheets, in scrapbooking sizes – 30 × 30cm (12 × 12in) or 20 × 20cm (8 × 8in) pieces – or in pads of various sizes.

Look out for different finishes and patterns, some examples of which are shown to the left, above and below. Patterned papers are very popular and come in every design you can think of. A touch of shimmer on card makes it special and using different textured card will also add interest and another dimension to your work.

Such an abundance of choice exists in terms of colour, feel, finish, weight and size that you should never have to compromise. Remember that rather than trying to replicate the materials I have used exactly for the projects, it is wise to keep a flexible approach. If you have something in your stash that would substitute just as well, do go ahead and use it.

ALL THE COLOURS OF CHRISTMAS

Papers and cards are available in a wide array of colours and the manufacturers are really challenging our ideas of traditional Christmas colours. It is possible to make all of your Christmas projects without ever resorting to red and green again. But I like to mix the traditional with the modern, and I hope some of the colour combinations I have used, and shown here, will inspire you in your selections.

Midnight Sky

Cool Ice Blue

Candy Pinks

Spring Greens

Christmas Brights

Hot Tropics

Peacock Colours

Jewel Tones

CHRISTMAS EMBELLISHMENTS

There is a huge range of decorative materials that you can choose from to add colour, pattern, texture and dimensional interest to your Christmas papercraft projects. Here I introduce the embellishments that I have used most often.

ADDING COLOUR AND PATTERN

There are lots of different ways to add colour and pattern to your background papers and card, so let's take a look at a few in more detail.

Pens

It is more than likely that you have a good collection of felt-tip pens in a range of rainbow colours, and you may even have a good collection of brush marker pens, but for Christmas papercrafts you need to invest in some really special pens to add sparkle and glitter to your designs. Glaze, opaque and metallic gel pens add a lustrous shimmer; the gelly roll pen dries to a glossy finish while the gelly glaze pen dries for a slightly raised effect. Metallic accents can also be added with a gilding pen or a multi-surface metallic liner pen.

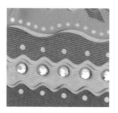

THIS DETAIL FROM THE PRESENT CARD (CHRISTMAS CARD LINE UP, PAGE 29) ILLUSTRATES HOW GEL PENS IN ASSORTED COLOURS HAVE BEEN USED TO HIGHLIGHT THE SHAPE OF DECORATIVELY CUT PAPER STRIPS WITH DOTTED PATTERNS.

A SIMPLE DOTTED BORDER IN A METALLIC GEL PEN, HAS BEEN USED TO OUTLINE THE LAYERED CARD MOTIFS THAT DECORATE THE FRONT OF THE BABY'S CHRISTMAS ALBUM (PAGE 72).

ON THE STAR GIFT BAG (PAGE 62) EVENLY SPACED DOTS, WORKED WITH A BLUE GELLY GLAZE PEN FOR A SLIGHTLY RAISED EFFECT, SWIRL ACROSS THE BACKGROUND PAPER. LARGER DOTS MADE WITH A GOLD MULTI-SURFACE LINER PEN ACCENT THE DRAWN PATTERN PERFECTLY.

Rubber Stamps

Rubber stamping is a quick and easy way to decorate paper and card, and the addition of a simple stamped snowflake design can really lift a background. Metallic inkpads are perfect for the festive season.

SNOWFLAKE MOTIFS STAMPED IN SILVER INK ACROSS A PALE BLUE CARD MAKE A GREAT BACKGROUND FOR THE SNOWMEN CASH CARD, PAGE 56.

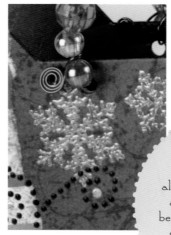

EMBOSSING POWDER CAN BE APPLIED TO A STAMPED IMAGE AND HEATED WITH A HEAT GUN TO CREATE A RAISED MOTIF AS THIS DETAIL FROM THE STAR GIFT BAG, PAGE 62, SHOWS.

TIP
No matter how short of time you are, always make sure stamps are thoroughly cleaned before putting away. Store stamps carefully as the rubber image can easily be damaged.

Adding Colour

Chalks and rubber stamping inkpads can be used to add accenting colour to your paper projects. This can be done in a number of ways: by using the inkpad to brush the colour directly onto the card; by sponging the chalk or ink on for a more broken up, cloudier effect; or by adding detail with an applicator.

A GOLD INKPAD HAS BEEN USED TO DECORATE THE CURVED PANELS OF THE CROWN BOX TRIO'S LARGEST BOX (PAGE 78). THE INK HAS BEEN SPONGED ON SO THAT A LITTLE OF THE CARD BASE COLOUR SHOWS THROUGH.

CHALKS HAVE BEEN USED EXTENSIVELY TO DECORATE THE FOLK ART BUNTING (PAGE 86). HERE CREAM CHALK HAS BEEN MORE SOLIDLY APPLIED WITH AN APPLICATOR FOR A SOLID TEXTURED EFFECT. ALTERNATIVELY, LOOSELY SPONGE CHALK ONTO A DIFFERENT COLOURED CARD BACKGROUND FOR A SOFT TEXTURED EFFECT.

ADDING TEXTURE AND DIMENSION

I love adding texture and dimension to my Christmas paper projects. If you can't use glitter and gemstones at this time of the year, when can you? Here are some of my favourite decorative embellishments.

Hole Punches

These come in many different sizes and they can be used to produce a shaped hole and a punched-out shape, either of which will look great in your projects. I am particularly fond of using small punches to create extra embellishments to fill project backgrounds, but larger punches can be handy when you need to make identical repeat images.

TIP
Make sure your work surface is firm and steady when punching as some punches are quite stiff. If a punch becomes blunt, punch through a piece of kitchen foil to sharpen it.

CIRCLE PUNCHES OF VARYING SIZES COULD BE USED AS AN ALTERNATIVE TO THE DIE CUTTING MACHINE TO MAKE THE BAUBLE CIRCLES FOR THE CASCADING LANTERN, PAGE 110.

Christmas Embellishments

Glitter

This comes loose or pre-mixed with glue and is available in opaque and transparent colours. The finer the glitter, the better the transparency and coverage. I love adding glitter embellishments and accents to my Christmas tree decorations so that they shimmer and sparkle in the fairy lights.

IN THE HANGING TREE DECORATION, PAGE 104, COLOURED EYELETS ARE USED TO HOLD THE GLITTER-DECORATED STARS IN PLACE, WHILE COLOURED BRADS PROVIDE ADDITIONAL DECORATION ON THE PAPER BACKGROUND.

Eyelets and Brads

These are useful for attaching paper or card to a background card, but they can also be purely decorative. Although the brads I use in this book are simple round ones, it is easy to find Christmas-shaped designs such as stars, trees and snowflakes. You can find details for fixing eyelets and brads on page 19.

IT CAN BE A BIT TRICKY FIXING LOOSE TINY GEMSTONES IN PLACE, BUT THE END OF A PRICKING TOOL OR A BRADAWL CAN BE USED FOR THE JOB.

Gemstones

Gemstones are the essential embellishment for adding sparkle to my festive projects. Flat-backed gems come in a range of shapes, sizes and colours, from tiny diamantés to star and heart motifs. You can buy them in self-adhesive strips, but I prefer to buy mine loose and to fix each individually with a strong clear adhesive as I find that they are less likely to fall off that way.

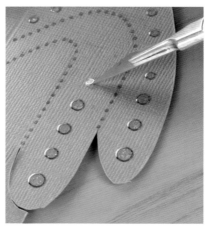

PEEL-OFF STICKERS PROVIDE A GOOD ALTERNATIVE TO GEMSTONES, AS CAN BE SEEN ON THIS DETAIL FROM THE ANGELIC MESSENGER CARD ON PAGE 42. TINY PEEL-OFFS ARE NO LESS TRICKY TO FIX IN PLACE THOUGH, AND A CRAFT KNIFE CAN HELP, BUT DO TAKE CARE.

Decorative Edged Scissors

These are scissors that have blades ready-cut with a decorative edge so that when the paper is cut a fancy edge is created. The pattern that will be cut is marked on the side of the scissors. I have used decorative edged scissors to create a jigsaw pieced paper to make cards in quantity that still manage to look individual (see Christmas Card Line Up, page 24).

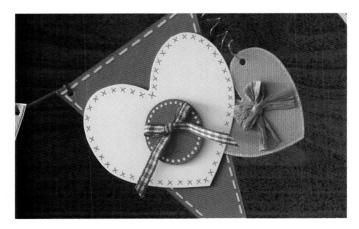

Ribbons and Braids

Ribbons and braids come in many different styles and sizes – plain or patterned, satin or sheer, narrow or wide, the choice is yours. Use ribbons to border edges, tie into decorative bows, or layer over each other for a more luxurious effect.

A DOUBLE-LOOP BOW TIED FROM NARROW PATTERNED RIBBON MAKES A LOVELY DECORATIVE EMBELLISHMENT (SEE PAGE 20 FOR STEP INSTRUCTIONS). THE RIBBON ENDS CAN BE CUT DIAGONALLY OR IN AN INVERTED 'V' FOR A MORE DECORATIVE FINISH. FOR A MORE RUSTIC LOOK, TIE BOWS FROM RAFFIA.

Embroidery Threads

Some simple stitching can add handmade charm to Christmas cards as can be seen with the Hand-stitched Stocking Card on page 48 where three simple stitches (cross stitch, running stitch and long stitch) are used to decorate bands of handmade paper. I have worked the stitches using stranded cotton (floss). This is made of six strands of thread, and you will need to separate out just three lengths of thread to sew with. If using the thread to tie decorative bows to stick to embellishing buttons, use all six thread strands.

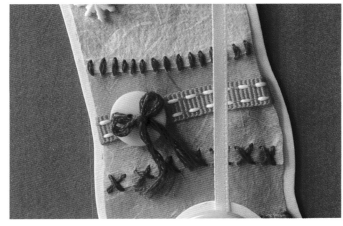

WHEN TYING BOWS WITH STRANDED COTTON (FLOSS) USE ALL SIX STRANDS; WHEN STITCHING, WORK WITH THREE STRANDS IN THE NEEDLE.

Buttons

Buttons are a great way to add embellishment to Christmas projects. You can buy special shaped Christmas buttons, or give old buttons a new lease of life with some ceramic paint. Always use a strong, clear adhesive to fix in place.

Beads and Wire

I like to incorporate luxurious beads into my Christmas projects. They can be strung onto cotton thread (Hanging Tree Decoration, page 104) or onto wire for a more rigid effect as with the beaded handle of the Star Gift Bag (page 62). Wire comes in a wide range of colours and it is available in different gauges – the higher the number the thinner the wire.

IN THE STAR GIFT BAG, PAGE 62, BEADS ARE STRUNG ONTO TURQUOISE CRAFT WIRE TO CREATE A LUXURIOUS HANDLE.

CLUSTERS OF SEASONAL BERRIES ARE WORKED BY THREADING A VARIETY OF BEADS ONTO LOOPS MADE FROM COPPER WIRE ON THE CHRISTMAS WREATH, PAGE 98.

BASIC TECHNIQUES

A few core techniques are outlined over the next few pages to help you to produce the most professional finish for your Christmas papercrafts.

CUTTING

Make the cleanest cuts with a flat, clean surface, a sharp craft knife and metal ruler, and a steady hand.

TIP
For large sheets, mark the cutting line with three pencil marks and cut about 20cm (8in). Keeping the knife in the paper, move your hand down the ruler, press firmly and continue cutting.

1 Using an HB pencil and metal ruler make two or three pencil marks on the card where you want the cutting line. With the card on a cutting mat, place the metal ruler along the line to be cut. It is best to stand when cutting with a craft knife. Press down on the ruler to hold it in place, while you draw the knife towards you in a single motion. Cut with the section you wish to use under the ruler, to ensure the knife will cut into the waste part if it slips.

2 Keep the blade of the craft knife at a 45° angle when cutting. Make sure you don't press too hard as you draw the knife across the paper or it will wrinkle and leave an uneven edge. If you are cutting thick card or paper, draw the blade across once without too much pressure, then cut again with more pressure to make the final cut.

Cutting Intricate Designs

When you are using a craft knife to cut an intricate design, do not try to cut the design in one stroke. Hold the knife in the cut and move the card before continuing. This will allow you to keep holding the knife at a comfortable angle to your body and will enable you to keep greater control as you cut. Alternatively use a knife with a rotating blade (see page 10).

SCORING AND FOLDING

Scoring paper and card allows it to be folded neatly and easily, giving a crisp, professional looking finish.

1 Make two pencil marks where you want the score line on the wrong side of the card or paper and line up the ruler with these marks. Draw an empty ball-point pen (or scoring tool) all the way along the line so the paper is indented. Press lightly on paper and more firmly on card. The scored line will become the inside of the fold.

2 Use both hands to fold the paper or card along the fold line. To make the fold line sharp, use a bone folder to press along the line. Although not shown for clarity, laying lightweight paper along the fold prevents shiny marks.

Making a Concertina Fold
To make the Snowmen Cash Card, page 56, you will need to fold your paper into a concertina. First, mark off the card along its long edge into three equal sections. Now score and fold down the two marked lines making the folds in opposite directions to create the concertina.

BRADS AND EYELETS

These decorative embellishments are easy to fix on card or paper when you know how. No special tools are required for brads but an eyelet punch, setter tool and hammer are needed to attach eyelets.

Fixing an Eyelet

1 Working on a cutting mat, use the eyelet punch and hammer to create a hole for the eyelet and place the eyelet upside down.

2 Turn the card over so that the wrong side is facing you and line up the hole with the eyelet. Use the setter tool and hammer to set the eyelet in your card. The eyelet is flattened so attaching it to the card.

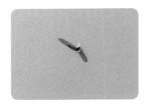

Fixing a Brad
To attach a brad simply cut a slit in the card, push the brad through, turn the card over and open out the legs pressing them flat.

TYING A DOUBLE LOOP BOW

For professional looking bows every time, follow these simple steps.

1 Form a loop at one end of the ribbon length and hold with one hand. Make a second loop of the same size a little further along the ribbon and hold in the other hand.

2 Take one loop and pass it over the top of the other loop. Pass this loop over and back through between the two loops.

3 Pull the loops tight. If the loops are too long, pull the ends of the ribbon to shorten.

4 Trim the ends to an inverted 'V' shape or cut on the diagonal to finish.

USING TEMPLATES

All the templates you require to make the projects featured in this book are on pages 118–126. Most are printed full size, but some need to be enlarged according to the percentage specified.

Using templates to copy an image that you might otherwise find difficult to scale up and draw is easy – just follow the simple instructions here.

TIP
If you have access to a computer and scanner at home, this is the quickest way to copy templates. You can increase the template size, print out onto lightweight card and save for future use.

1 Use an HB pencil and tracing paper to trace the chosen image from the template, or photocopy the image onto paper. Cut around the image using scissors.

2 Place the paper template on scrap card. Hold the paper in place and draw around the paper template using a pencil.

3 Cut out the image from the cardboard to form the template. Discard the paper template, as this will not be sturdy enough. You can label and store your cardboard templates in plastic sleeves in a ring-binder for future use.

MAKING A BASIC ENVELOPE

It is easy to make an envelope to fit the exact size of your cards, and this way you can ensure that card and envelope coordinate perfectly.

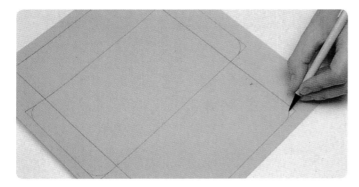

1 First make a template of your card. Measure the card front and draw onto scrap paper adding 3mm (⅛in) to each edge. At the top edge, draw the flap half the depth of the front. At the bottom edge, draw the envelope back taking 2cm (¾in) off the depth. Draw a tab at each side of the front 2.5cm (1in) wide and draw a curve at each corner.

2 Cut out and use this template to draw your envelope onto the wrong side of your chosen paper or thin card. Cut out, score and fold along the lines. Fold the side tabs in.

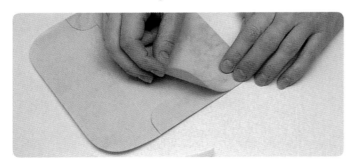

3 Apply double-sided tape along the side edges of the back, peel off the backing and stick over the side tabs. Insert your card and tuck the flap inside the envelope.

MAKING A BOX ENVELOPE

If sending the 3D Tree Card, page 36, by post you will need to make a box envelope to accommodate its depth. For added protection, glue a piece of bubble wrap in the lid and wrap the card in tissue paper.

1 First make a template. Measure the card front and draw it on scrap paper adding 3mm (⅛in) to each edge. Draw a side to the box along each edge that is the depth of the finished greeting card plus 3mm (⅛in). Add a 1.5cm (⅝in) wide tab to both ends of two opposite box sides and draw a slanted end to each tab. Cut out the template and use to cut the base of the box from card.

2 Score and fold along all the marked lines. Fold the box sides upwards. Glue the tabs under the end of the opposite box sides with double-sided tape. To make a lid, you will need to make a second template, adding 2mm (¹⁄₁₆in) to each edge of the base.

GREETINGS

Christmas is just the excuse you need for indulging in one of your favourite papercrafting activities – card making. What better way than a beautiful handmade card to wish friends and family the best the season has to offer.

These projects will provide you with ideas for making cards that stand out from the rest – quite literally in the case of the simple paper sculpted **3D Tree Card** and the **Angelic Messenger**, a pop-out card that can be easily posted – while **Tags Galore** has ideas for making your gifts the stars beneath the tree.

You may not be short on card-making ideas at Christmas, but the chances are you will be short on time. **Christmas Card Line Up** has a great idea for making card multiples that still manage to be different from each other and the decorative detailing of the **Hand-stitched Stocking** can be worked during those long winter evenings in front of the fire.

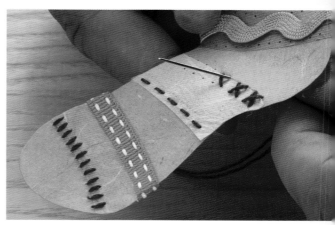

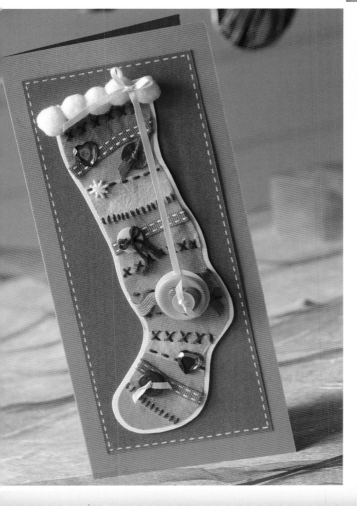

Christmas Card Line Up

Even though you may be pushed for time in the run up to Christmas, it is still possible to make beautifully detailed hand-crafted cards. I have devised a simple production line technique to enable you to quickly create multiples of this intricate star-topped Christmas tree design. The materials listed overleaf are sufficient to make ten cards in all.

The Christmas tree triangles are cut from a decorated card base made by piecing together decoratively cut paper strips in assorted vibrant colours. The card blanks can be cut from different colours of cardstock to ring the changes, and you can spend as much or as little time as you choose finishing off each card by hand, adding decorative gemstones and gel pen detailing.

LINEUP, LINEUP

No two cards will look exactly the same as the tree triangles are cut from different areas of the decorated card base, which has been hand-finished with gemstones and gel pen detailing.

You will need

✳ Nine sheets A4 (US letter) heavyweight paper, assorted colours

✳ One sheet A5 light green card

✳ Cardstock, assorted colours

✳ Three different patterned decorative-edged scissors

✳ Glaze and opaque gel pens, white and assorted colours

✳ Gemstones and star-shaped gems

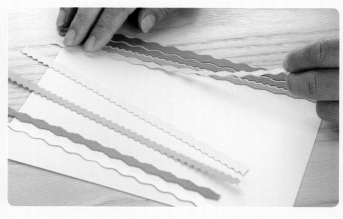

1 Use the decorative-edged scissors to cut 21 cm (8¼ in) long strips from the heavyweight paper sheets, varying the width from 3mm to 1cm (⅛ in to ⅜ in). For extra variety ensure that some paper strips have different cut patterns along both edges. Lay out the cut paper strips on your work surface in piles of the same colour.

2 Select a wide decorative-edged paper strip and glue at one long edge of the light green A5 card. Find a different coloured paper strip to match the cut pattern of the stuck down strip and glue it alongside, leaving a 1mm (1/32 in) gap between the two paper strips. Continue adding different coloured strips of paper in the same way, checking every third piece that the lines are still running parallel to the edge of the base card. Do not worry that some paper strips have to overlap the short edges of the card in order to fit into the 'jigsaw' as the edges of the finished paper-strip decorated card will not be used. Continue to piece the paper strips together until the base card is completely full.

TIP
To make the cutting of the paper strips even quicker, you could use a rotary cutter with three interchangeable decorative blades. If you are intending to make all your Christmas cards using this design, it would be a sensible investment.

3 Mark along each long side of the decorated base card at 6cm (2³⁄₈in) intervals, ignoring the first 1cm (³⁄₈in) or so where the paper strips may overlap or fall short of the card edge. Use a soft pencil to join the marks diagonally to create large diamonds. Draw a line through the middle of the diamonds to give you ten triangles. Use a sharp craft knife and a steel ruler to neatly cut the marked triangles out, discarding the excess pieces at the sides. Check that the paper strips are stuck down at the edges of each triangle.

TIP
A similar effect can be achieved even more quickly by cutting triangles from pre-printed striped paper. Do glue the paper onto thin card first to ensure the shape is cut cleanly, otherwise bent corners may spoil the look.

4 To make each card blank, cut a piece of card 10.5 × 21cm (4¹⁄₈ × 8¹⁄₄in), score down the centre and fold in half. Glue a 9.5cm (3³⁄₄in) square in a complementary colour to the centre of the card blank. Mount a stripy tree in the centre using small 3D foam pads, and making sure that the base of the triangle is parallel to the card square.

TIP
Take your time when building up the decorative detail on your card. Limit yourself to three or four pen colours, and remember that sometimes less is more. Do not spoil this simple design by over embellishing it.

5 Use the gel pens to add detail to the stripy tree with lines of dots that either follow the curves of the decorative edges or run straight through the middle of the paper strips. Start by decorating every third strip of paper and add more detail as you feel necessary.

6 Use a fine white opaque gel pen to draw a 'stitched' border around the background card square to lift the whole design. For extra special detailing, glue five or six small gemstones to one of the wider paper strips and a star-shaped gem to the tree top, using a strong clear adhesive to hold the stones in place.

A BAND OF IDEAS

Why not experiment with using other stripy shaped motifs? Try a simple square for a ribbon-wrapped gift (above and described below), or make and glue together small stripy diamond shapes for a six-pointed star.

1 Make a stripy paper sheet following steps 1 and 2 on page 26.

2 Measure out a 5cm (1⅞in) square onto the stripy paper sheet and cut out. Glue to a 7cm (2¾in) square of gold mirror card, as shown above.

3 Add decorative detailing to the paper strips using the gel pens, and, for a finishing touch, add a ribbon bow to the top of the present. Make a card blank (see step 4, page 27) and mount the present square on top.

You will need

* One sheet A4 (US letter) deckle-edged, gold-mirror card
* Nine sheets A4 (US letter) heavyweight paper, assorted colours
* One sheet A5 card
* Cardstock, assorted colours
* Three different patterned decorative-edged scissors
* Glaze and opaque gel pens, assorted colours
* Ribbon bow

TIP
For a completely different look, use the stripy sheet to decorate the front of a card blank. Cut a tree, present or star shape from gold mirror card and fix on top. Pen work can then be added to the background as before.

Tags Galore

Nothing finishes off a neatly wrapped present better than a hand-crafted tag. When time is short, tags are so quick to make and they are a great way to use the scraps you have been saving from your card-making projects all year round. An exuberantly decorated tag will add an eye-catching focus to a gift simply wrapped in a plain or metallic paper and tied with coloured string or ribbon.

It is fun to see what designs you can come up with on such a small area, but the key to success is taking the time to select materials that complement each other. Black and white works with just about everything and even the smallest addition of a bright colour, such as the pink used here, will stop it looking too severe.

RIBBON DETAIL
Gift ribbons have inspired this tag design. Lengths of cut ribbon in varying widths draw the eye to the handmade snowflake topper.

You will need

✳ Small pieces plain and textured pale pink card, textured deep pink card, and silver metallic card

✳ Black and white patterned paper

✳ Gauze ribbon in shades of pink, varying widths

✳ White and sparkly pink metallic gel pens

✳ Pink glitter

✳ Pink and silver gemstones or small sequins

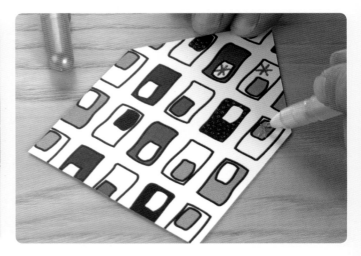

1 Cut a piece of pink card 7 × 10cm (2¾ × 4in) and mark the centre of the short edge. Measure down the long sides by 4cm (1½in) and join the three marks to form an arrowhead. Cut along the lines to make the pointed end of the tag.

2 Cover the front of the tag with black and white geometric patterned paper and trim the edges neatly. Punch a small hole at the top of the point for stringing. Use a sparkly pink gel pen to add simple snowflakes and dots to some areas of the pattern, avoiding the bottom left of the tag.

TIP
Remember to leave one side of the tag uncovered to write your message on. If you only have white card, don't despair – you can always cover the message side with a pretty plain paper.

3 Cut a 5cm (2in) diameter circle from pink textured card. Turn the circle over and fix short strips of double-sided tape around the edge. Cut approximately eighteen 4cm (1½in) lengths from the pink gauze ribbons, aiming for a good variety of colours and widths. Neatly trim one end of each ribbon into an inverted 'V' shape. Fix the untrimmed ribbon ends to the tape so that they fan out from the centre of the circle.

4 Cut a 4.8cm (1⅝in) diameter circle from silver metallic card. Use a pencil and ruler to divide the circle into six segments, marking faintly. Carefully trace over the marked lines with a white gel pen, adding an arrowhead and dot to the ends of each line. Sprinkle pink glitter onto the ink, working quickly before it dries. Shake off the excess.

5 Using the template on page 119, draw a stylized snowflake onto pale pink card and cut out carefully with small sharp scissors. Glue the pink snowflake to the centre of the circle so that the points lay between the lines of glitter.

TIP
Do make sure that the white gel ink has completely dried before gluing on the snowflake motif. Use a fine paintbrush to brush away any stray glitter.

6 Fix the ribbon circle onto the bottom left side of the
patterned tag using 3D foam tape and taking care that no
ribbon ends are tucked underneath. Glue the silver circle to the
ribbon circle. Use a strong clear glue to add extra gemstone or
sequin embellishments to the snowflake.

TIP
You can easily
upgrade the snowflake
tag to a card embellishment
by fixing it to the front of a plain
card blank with a few 3D foam
pads. Place the tag at an angle
and add a handwritten message
for a quick and easy solution
to those last-minute
greetings.

TIP
Ribbons are a great
way to bring focus to the
decorative motif. Here the
stripy grosgrain ribbon tails
draw the eye to a simple paper
pattern band that has been
decorated with a small
chocolate coin.

TEDDY TAG

A baby's first Christmas can be marked by making this special tag. The fantastic layered star motif can be removed easily and a simple hanging cord added to create a treasured tree decoration for Christmases to come.

You will need

❋ Small pieces of yellow, light blue and gold mirror card

❋ Star rubber stamp and gold inkpad

❋ Two blue tones glaze gel pens and opaque blue gel pen

❋ One teddy button and five gold diamond gems

1 Following the instructions in step 1, page 32, cut a gift tag from the yellow card. Use the star rubber stamp to decorate the tag with a turn and repeat pattern. Colour in the stamped design with the glaze gel pens.

2 Use the star template, page 119, to cut two stars from the gold mirror card and one star from the light blue card. Trim the light blue star so that it is slightly smaller and glue it to one of the gold stars. Use a strong clear glue to fix the teddy button to the centre and decorate the star points with the gold diamond gems.

3 Use 3D foam pads to attach the remaining gold star to the centre of the tag. Glue the decorated star on top positioning carefully to create a ten-point star. Use the blue opaque pen to decorate the star points of the gold star below.

TIP
When making tags for children's gifts, consider their age and their favourite things to help inspire your choice of decorative motif.

35

3D Tree Card

The idea of paper sculpture can be daunting to the novice papercrafter, yet one of the most basic of all three-dimensional shapes is the simple cone. This eye-catching 3D tree design is created from a series of cones made in decreasing sizes and stacked up on the front of a plain card blank. The cones are shaped from semicircles cut from several sheets of paper bought as a colour-themed pack. Coordinated papers such as these are ideal for creating variety in the tree layers whilst ensuring that the whole design pulls together.

It is best if a 3D card can be hand-delivered, but if this is not possible you will find instructions for making a simple box envelope on page 21 to ensure that your 3D card keeps its shape perfectly.

TREE SKIRTS

Before shaping the paper semicircles into cones, the edges are finely cut and curled to create a fringed border to give the effect of dense branches. Each layer is decorated with gemstones to catch the light.

You will need

❋ Pack of coordinating patterned papers with a minimum of four designs

❋ 10.5cm (4⅛in) square plain cream card

❋ Four pink metallic eyelets and eyelet setting tools

❋ 14cm (5½in) square light green card blank

❋ Small pink gemstones and a larger star-shaped gem

1 Take three different patterns of paper and draw a line across 1cm (⅜in) from the edge of each. Using this line as a base, take a compass and draw a 5cm (2in) semicircle and a 2cm (¾in) diameter semicircle on the first piece of paper. Draw 4cm (1½in) and 1cm (⅜in) diameter circles on the second piece of paper and a 3cm (1⅛in) diameter semicircle on the third. Cut out all of the pieces.

2 Use the compass to draw a line inside the curve of each semicircle to make a guideline for cutting the fringe. On the 5cm (2in) semicircle draw a 3.5cm (1⅜in) diameter curve; on the 4cm (1½in) semicircle a 2.75cm (1⅙in) diameter curve; on the 3cm (1⅛in) semicircle a 2cm (¾in) diameter curve; on the 2cm (¾in) semicircle a 1.25cm (½in) diameter curve; and on the 1cm (⅜in) semicircle a 5mm (³⁄₁₆in) diameter curve. Fold each piece along the straight pencil line and snip a right-angle triangle in the centre of the folded area.

TIP
Do take care when cutting the fringing to avoid making the cuts too close together. If the fringe is too fine you'll risk accidentally tearing pieces off when curling over the scissors.

3 To create a fringed border, use small sharp scissors to snip from the edge of each semicircle to the marked inner curve. It helps to first snip at the halfway point, then quarters, eighths, sixteenths, etc., so that each cut points towards the middle of the semicircle. Ideally the resulting fringes will be 1–2mm (¹⁄₃₂–³⁄₃₂ in) wide.

TIP
Mistakes do happen and you might find that you end up curling the fringing in the wrong direction. This can be easily rectified by flipping the semicircle over and recurling a couple of times in the opposite way.

4 Take each semicircle and carefully pull the fringing between your thumb and one blade of a pair of scissors to gently curl the fringe. As long as the patterned side of the paper runs over the blade the fringe will curl the correct way when the cones are assembled.

5 Draw a line down the centre of the square of cream card. Mark a point 2cm (¾in) down from the top. Trim down the folded tabs of the smallest semicircle to about 4mm (⁵/₃₂in) wide and glue the two sides together to make a flattened cone with a right-angled point. Fix this cone to the card square so that the point covers the pencil mark you have just made.

6 Take the 2cm (¾in) semicircle and shape into a cone. Glue this inside the first cone, making sure that the cone point sits on the pencil line to keep the tree shape straight. Continue adding the cones in order of size. Once completed, gently flatten each cone a little so the undersides cannot be seen when the card is held upright.

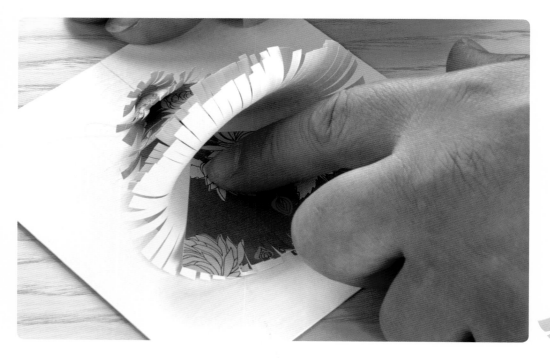

7 Cut a quarter circle 5cm (2in) in diameter from the third piece of paper and fringe the edge as before. Glue this inside the bottom cone to cover the folded tabs and neaten the base of the tree. Fluff up the fringes with your fingertips and carefully erase all pencil marks.

8 To make a coordinating border, take the fourth piece of patterned paper and cut four 5mm (³⁄₁₆in) wide strips of paper each measuring 10.5cm (4in) long. Stick the strips to the edges of the square and neaten each corner by cutting the ends to a 45° angle.

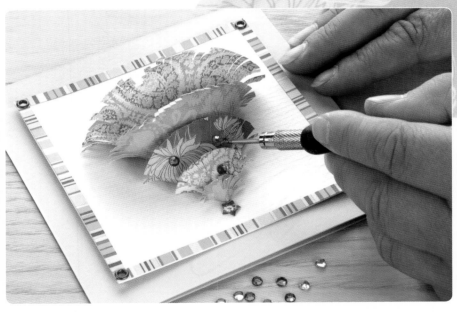

9 Fit a pink metallic eyelet into the middle of each mitred corner (see page 19).

10 Mount the card square onto the larger square card blank using 3D foam pads to add more depth to the design. Use a strong clear glue to attach a star-shaped gem to the top of the tree and a scattering of small coordinating gemstones to the tree layers.

Angelic Messenger

One way to guarantee that your Christmas cards really stand out on the mantelpiece is to make sure they really do 'stand out'! Whether you're giving them by hand or popping them in the post it can be difficult to put an extra dimensional card into an envelope, so I've designed this serene angel card to fold flat like a normal card for easy delivery.

Clever cutting and scoring means that the figure will pop out from the background with a simple fold and the card stays in this position with tuck in tabs. Once you've mastered the mechanics behind the design you can create a number of variations to fly out to all of your friends.

SPARKLING IN FLIGHT
The clever combination of shimmery, metallic and holographic materials gives this angel a subtle but suitably angelic glow.

You will need

❋ One sheet A5 textured, pearlized lilac card
❋ Small pieces of shimmery, cream card;
  gold metallic card; matt, pale pink card
❋ 18 x 14.5cm (7 x 5¾in) white parchment
❋ Holographic peel off circles in three sizes
❋ Mauve and gold metallic gel pens
❋ Fine line felt-tip pens

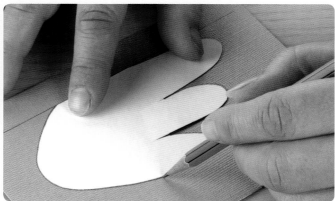

1 Fold the lilac card into an A6 card blank. Make a faint pencil line down the long side, 1.5cm (½in) from the edge. Place the straight part of the wing template (page 118) on this line so that the shape falls centrally on the card and trace around this in pencil, as shown above, then remove the template. While the card is still folded, carefully cut around the wing shape with a sharp craft knife, pressing hard enough to cut through both layers. Do not cut the straight part of the wing marked with a dotted line on the template on page 118.

2 Open the card out and score lines where the wings are still attached to the card. Fold the wings over and score two more lines down the card to divide it into four long rectangles. Fold the end quarters into the middle to ensure the wings are level and stand out from the parameters of the card.

3 Remove any remaining pencil marks with a soft eraser to avoid damaging the pearlized surface of the card. To make an insert, fold the white parchment in half. Fix to the centre fold of the card with narrow double-sided tape and fold the edges to the middle, parallel to the quarter folds of the card.

4 Lay the folded card in front of you with the wings uppermost, and make two marks on the right hand, cut side, 1cm (⅜in) from the corners and 1.5cm (½in) long. Cut two slots as shown above, parallel to the cut edge of the card using these marks as a guide. Enlarge the cuts slightly by cutting again as close as possible to each one.

5 Draw a set of matching lines on the left hand side and cut the side of the card 5mm (³⁄₁₆in) from the edge, as shown above. Using these as a guide, draw two tab shapes that will fit into the slots on the other side. Cut the tabs and fold along the lines that are parallel to the edge. Check the tabs slot easily into the slits and trim if necessary. The card should now stand up as a triangular shape with the wings sticking out from the sides.

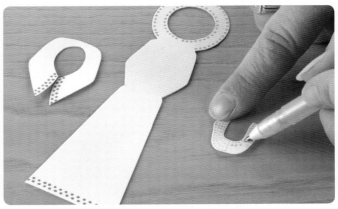

6 Lay the card down again with the edges folded to the middle and the wings lying flat, as shown above. Lightly sketch lines to indicate the curve of a wing and ensure the design is mirrored on the opposite side. Decorate the shorter lines with a series of small dots using a mauve metallic gel pen. Follow the longer lines with three sizes of holographic peel-off circles, using the larger ones for the tips and decreasing the size as you move up the wing. Allow the gel pen to dry completely before gently rubbing out the pencil lines with a soft eraser.

7 Use the angel template (page 118) to trace around the body, sleeves and hair onto the cream card. Cut out each piece with small sharp scissors or a craft knife. Rub out any pencil marks and decorate the edges of the dress and sleeves with a double line of dots using a mauve metallic gel pen. Add detail to the halo and hair in the same way with a gold gel pen and leave to dry.

TIP
Always test the gel ink is dry before rubbing away the pencil lines. If in doubt, cut a small sliver from your eraser and carefully rub away between the dots to avoid smudging.

45

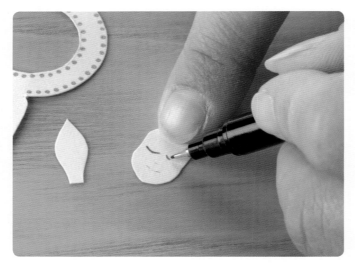

8 Cut the face and hand shapes (page 118) from a scrap of pale pink card. Draw the eyelids, nose and mouth onto the lower part of the face using fine line felt-tip pens. For the cheeks, add coloured circles in a slightly darker pink than the card colour on either side of the nose.

9 Assemble the angel by gluing the hands to the underside of the two sleeves. Glue the top part of the sleeves just below the halo on the body shape. Use 3D foam pads to secure the ends of the sleeves to the centre of the body so that they stand proud of the dress. Fix a small circle of gold card behind the halo. Glue the hair in position onto the face and fix this to the centre of the halo with a 3D foam pad.

10 On the reverse of the completed angel place four foam pads down the centre, keeping away from the top and bottom of the figure. Slot the card together again and fix the angel to the uppermost part of the card without the pads obstructing the slots. The card can now be unfolded to post and easily re-assembled by the recipient.

TIP
As an alternative to the slot assembly you could hold the edges of the card in place with paperclips while fixing the angel to the front, then send it with two small pieces of double-sided tape in place of the tabs.

WINGS OF A DOVE

You will need

* 10 x 11cm (4 x 4⅜in) blue card blank
* Small pieces of shimmery white card, and yellow card
* Blue gemstones
* Black fine line felt-tip pen

Experiment with shorter card blanks and different wing designs to make variation fold-out cards. This striking dove card is a perfect example.

1 Trace the wing template (page 119) and make the card base in the same way as steps 1–3 on page 44, but cutting the wings to leave a 1mm (1/16in) border all the way around the guideline.

2 Cut two wings from shimmery white card, one reversed, to the same size as the template. Curl the tips slightly over a scissor blade before gluing the solid part of the shape to the card. Trace the body template on page 119 and cut from the shimmery white card.

Cut out a beak from yellow card and glue in place, then draw on the eye with the black fine line felt-tip pen.

3 Fold and glue narrow strips of contrasting card to the top and bottom edges of the card and decorate with the blue gemstones. The card is held in the triangular shape with small pieces of double-sided tape as the off-centre dove's body would not hide the tab and slot method.

Hand–Stitched Stocking

The stocking is a popular Christmas motif and by choosing bright, contemporary colours it is possible to give this traditional favourite a fresh, stylish spin. Inspired by the hand-stitched stockings of yesteryear, I have added a modern twist with colourful ribbons, button charms and a pompom trim. The handmade papers used are a perfect base for stitching onto, as they are supple enough to allow a needle to pass through easily but strong enough to withstand the amount of handling required for this sampler-style sewing.

Most of the decorative work for this card can be done away from your workstation and you'll only need a flat surface for the final assembly and to add the pen detailing.

ALL STITCHED UP

Three simple stitches are used to decorate the handmade paper strips – running stitch, cross stitch and straight stitch. If you can't find store-bought ribbons like these, add white running stitch to plain ribbon.

You will need

❋ 18 × 7cm (7 × 2¾in) orange handmade silk-fibre paper

❋ Small pieces of pink handmade silk-fibre paper in three different shades

❋ Orange ric-rac braid, narrow pink and orange grosgrain ribbons

❋ One skein deep pink stranded cotton (floss) and size 22 embroidery needle

❋ 18 × 7cm (7 × 2¾in) white card

❋ 21 × 10cm (8¼ × 4in) orange card blank

❋ 18.5 × 8cm (7⅜ × 3⅛in) pink paper

❋ Fine-tip white gel pen

❋ Embellishments: pompom trim; narrow satin ribbons, white, red and purple; buttons, assorted sizes, shapes and colours; heart-shaped gemstones

1 Use the template on page 123 to cut out the stocking from the orange silk-fibre paper and lay flat. Cut the pink silk-fibre papers into wavy strips approximately 1–2cm (⅜–¾in) wide. Glue the pink strips across the stocking, alternating the shades and leaving 5mm–1cm (³⁄₁₆–¾in) of the orange base paper showing between them.

2 Trim the ends of the pink strips to the stocking outline and ensure that all the edges are firmly stuck down. Cut the grosgrain ribbons and ric-rac braid into 6cm (2⅜in) lengths. Stick the ribbons to the stocking using double-sided tape and following the pattern of the pink paper strips. Fold the ends of the ribbon under the stocking to avoid fraying.

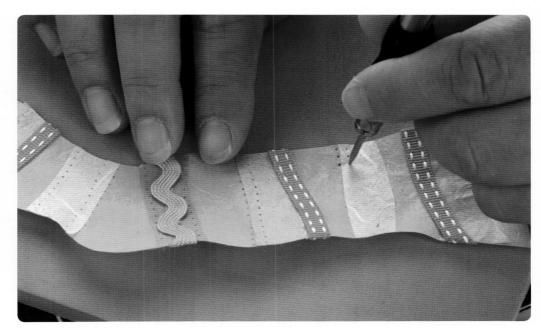

3 Place the striped stocking onto a soft work mat or phone directory and use a pricking tool or a darning needle to prick out guideline holes for the stitching. For running stitch, prick out a single line of regularly spaced holes about 2mm (3/32 in) from the paper strip edge. For cross stitch and straight stitch, prick out two parallel lines of holes, one resting on the paper strip edge and the other about 4mm (5/32 in) away.

TIP
Stitch with thread lengths no longer than 30cm (12in). If the thread is twisting as you work, simply hold the thread in the eye of the needle and let the stocking dangle down, to untwist itself.

4 Thread the needle with three strands of stranded cotton (floss) and knot the ends. Using the pre-pricked holes as a guide and starting at the stocking toe, take the needle up from the back of the stocking and stitch neatly through the paper layers from edge to edge. Try not to pull the thread too tightly or the paper will pucker. As you complete each stitched row, cut off the thread to leave a 2cm (¾in) tail, and tape the thread end securely to the stocking back. Continue to stitch each row in this way until you reach the stocking top.

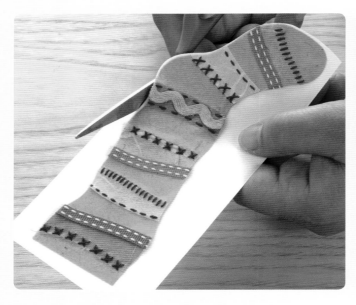

5 Apply glue to the back of the stocking with a dry glue stick so that the paper does not wrinkle too much. Fix the stocking to the white card and carefully smooth down flat to avoid pulling the stitching or ribbons. Use sharp paper scissors to cut around the shape leaving a 2mm (³/₃₂ in) border of white card showing.

6 Cut a piece of white pompom trim about five bobbles wide. Use double-sided tape to fix the pompom trim braid to the top edge of the stocking, gathering it up slightly to fit the width of the shape. Put a dot of strong, high-tack glue on each pompom; leave for 30 seconds to increase the tack, then flip the pompoms back over, pushing together slightly to hide the braid.

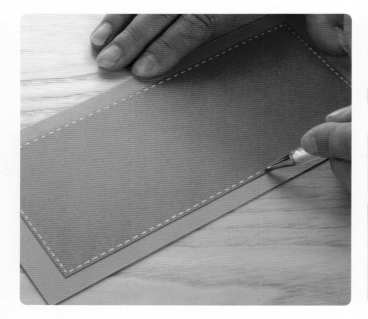

7 Stick the pink paper rectangle to the centre of the card blank. Use the white gel pen to add a line of fake stitching around the edge of the pink panel.

8 To decorate the buttons, thread narrow satin ribbon or stranded cotton (floss) through the buttonholes and tie in a knot or a bow at the front of the button. Use a pair of sharp scissors to trim the ribbon ends diagonally to prevent fraying.

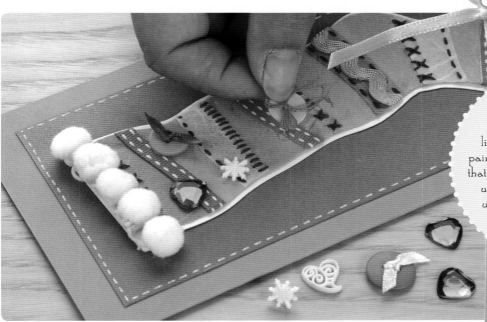

TIP
To give old buttons a new lease of life, paint with a ceramic paint. You will need to ensure that they are touch dry before using, but you can speed up the process by gently waving a heat gun over them.

9 Place 3D foam pads on the back of the stocking and fix it to the middle of the card blank leaving an equal space at the top and bottom. Use a strong clear glue to randomly fix the decorated buttons onto the stocking front and add a further selection of heart-shaped gemstones and motif-style button charms. Limit yourself to seven or eight items or you will find the card becomes overcrowded and the stitch detailing will be lost.

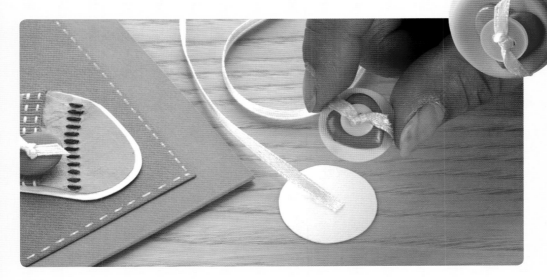

10 To make the hanging button charm, stack three buttons together in order of size so the smallest is on the top and tie together as before with a narrow white ribbon. Cut a circle of white card slightly larger than the bottom button and fix one end of a 20cm (8in) length of white satin ribbon to its centre. Glue the button stack over the top of the ribbon end to secure it. Tie a neat bow at the other end of the ribbon about 9cm (3½in) from the charm and fix to the side of the pompom trim with strong clear glue to allow the charm to swing freely.

GIVING

The giving and receiving of gifts at Christmas is one of the greatest of the season's pleasures. But how do you make the presents you give stand out from all the rest? A special papercrafted wrapping could be just the answer you are looking for.

The cute **Snowmen Cash Card** provides the perfect way to make store vouchers look interesting, while the sumptuously decorated **Star Gift Bag** with its beaded handles is ideal for jewellery gifts. And in **Crown Box Trio** I share with you a super box design that can easily be adapted for any size of gift. The making of a photo album, sharing the memories of another year, is explored in the **Baby's Christmas Album** chapter.

Why limit your presents to Christmas day? With the **Advent Calendar** you can drip-feed mini presents right up to the big day itself.

Snowmen Cash Card

Gift vouchers make ideal presents for family and friends who live far away, as they are easy to post and the lucky recipients can look forward to treating themselves in the New Year sales. Unfortunately the stores that offer these vouchers quite often provide uninspiring cards to accompany them. Remedy this situation by making a one-off designer card that has a slip-in pocket to hold a voucher – it will look great on the windowsill long after the voucher has been spent.

This card design involves building up paper shapes, layering and matting onto a tri-fold card to give an incredible 3D effect that's so easy to achieve and which will ensure that your loved ones receive a gift to treasure.

SNOWMEN SALUTE

The delightful snowmen figures are created by layering paper shapes onto the background card, which is then cut away to reveal the rubber-stamped panel beneath. The detailing is so much fun to make!

You will need

❄ One sheet A4 (US letter) light blue card
❄ One sheet A4 (US letter) white textured pearlescent card
❄ Snowflakes rubber stamp
❄ Silver pigment ink
❄ 3 × 21cm (1⅛ × 8¼in) pale blue textured pearlescent card
❄ Small pieces of brown textured pearlescent card
❄ Pale blue and white opaque gel pens
❄ Black and red gelly roll pens
❄ Mid-blue brush pen
❄ Scraps of orange card and brilliant green paper
❄ Small holly sprig punch

1 Score the light blue card into three equal sections, concertina fold (see page 19) and open out flat. Ink up the snowflakes rubber stamp with silver pigment ink and randomly stamp the design over the centre section of the card. Use pale blue and white opaque gel pens to fill in any empty areas of the background with a dotted pattern for an all-over design.

TIP
To ensure nice crisp edges on the card blank, run along the scored fold lines with a bone folder.

2 Re-fold the card blank so that the third facing you has the fold at its base. Cut the pale blue pearlescent card into gently rolling hills. Glue this along the fold line to make the ground for the snowmen to stand on. Use the templates on page 118 to cut the pieces for the three snowmen from the white pearlescent card. Begin assembling the figures by positioning the largest body pieces close to the bottom of the card at fairly equal distances apart.

3 Continue to build up the snowmen by overlapping the smaller body pieces and placing the heads at the top. Use sharp scissors to cut around the completed snowmen leaving a 7mm (9/32 in) border around the hills at the base and a 2mm (3/32 in) border around the figures themselves. Run the side of a mid-blue brush pen along the cut edges of the outlines so they stand out a little better from the revealed stamped background. Use the white pen to make a pattern of closely spaced dots on the landscape's border, so that it looks like freshly fallen snow.

4 Using the templates on page 118 cut six twig arms (two of each) from the brown pearlescent card and glue in place on the bodies of the snowmen. To make the end figures look as if they are facing inwards, stick one arm to the back of each figure. Cut three small triangles of orange card for the carrot noses and glue in place, as shown on page 58. Add the facial details and buttons with a black gelly roll pen, which will dry to a glossy finish.

5 Use the templates on page 118 to cut three hats from the pearlescent brown card. To decorate the hats, make a hatband by using the white opaque gel pen to mark on three rows of small dots. Use the punch to cut sprigs of holly from the brilliant green paper and add red gelly roll pen spots for the berries. When the ink is completely dry glue the holly sprigs to the side of each hat.

TIP
To make a smaller holder for the credit-card style of voucher, follow the same instructions but use a 10.5 x 21cm (long half US letter) sheet of card and a single, forward-facing snowman.

6 Place a double thickness of 3D foam tape above each snowman's head, leaving approximately a 1mm (1/32 in) clearance. Decide how to position the hats, and when you are happy press down firmly onto the tape. The hat brims keep the snowmen's heads in place so that a voucher can be slipped behind the cut-out figures.

SANTA'S SPECIAL DELIVERY

TIP
Now you
know how, why not
explore making your own
variations, such as Christmas
trees held in place with stars,
or rows of presents topped
with cut-out rosettes.

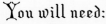

You will need:
* One sheet A4 (US letter) green card
* Gold inkpad
* Small pieces of red, pink and black card, and white textured pearlescent card
* One large and two small paper fasteners
* One sheet A5 Christmas patterned paper

Many stores now use a plastic swipe card, so here is a smaller card to present this in. A triangular slot is cut into the front to hold a token in a separate decorative envelope.

1 Fold the A4 green card in half and cut to make a triangular blank. Follow the shape of the card to mark a triangular tab measuring 2.5cm (1in) in from the sides and the base. Open the card and cut along the two side lines. Use the gold inkpad to decorate the edges of the front of the card.

2 To make a large Santa decoration to hide the tab, use the templates on page 119. Cut the base body and jacket from red card. Fix the jacket to the body with 3D foam pads. The white fur trim is cut from white pearlescent card and incorporates a circular hood to fix the face behind. Cut the hair and beard from white pearlescent card and curl its edges over the blade of a pair of scissors. Fix to the front of the hood with 3D foam pads. Colour the face with a little pink chalk for rosy cheeks and add the facial details. Fix the face behind the hood and position the trim onto the jacket. Add the black boots, gloves and belt, decorated with gold brads, then glue the white cuffs and hat bobble in place. Finally, mount the figure over the cut out triangle on the card base.

3 Make an envelope (see page 21) from Christmas patterned paper for the credit card voucher. Place the envelope in the tab behind Santa.

Star Gift Bag

Small precious gifts such as jewellery demand an extra special wrapping and I have designed a luxurious gift bag that is perfect for the job. A star-shaped papier mâché bag blank is the starting point for this project. Its paper surface takes glue and paint smoothly, and the thickness of the board used allows it to be stamped and heat embossed without distorting its shape. Beaded handles are added so that the bag can be hung from the tree until it is ready to be given. Wrap the gift in tissue paper to match and pop inside.

For this altered art project, the blank is first covered in a base paper; then découpage, pen work and rubber stamping techniques are used to produce a beautifully intricate design on the bag front.

BEAD-DAZZLED!

Beautiful crystals and pearlized beads that match the colours of the papers used are threaded onto coloured wire to make strong handles.

You will need

❄ Papier mâché star-shaped bag blank

❄ Patterned papers in tones of blue

❄ Snowflake rubber stamps; gold pigment ink;
   gold pearlescent embossing powder; heat gun

❄ Blue gelly glaze pen and gold multisurface
   metallic liner pen

❄ Crystal, metallic and pearlescent beads,
   assorted colours

❄ Turquoise craft wire

❄ Round-nosed pliers

1 To cover the front and back panels of the star-shaped bag blank, choose a mid tone patterned paper with an all over distressed or woven design. Glue one side of the star and place onto the wrong side of the paper. Use a craft knife to cut around the star leaving a 1cm (⅜in) border. Clip into the corners to make flaps and glue these to the bag gusset. Repeat for the other side. Cover the bag gusset with a strip of paper that measures its exact width.

2 Choose some lighter coloured papers that will coordinate with the background paper - stripes and wording styles work well. Tear the paper into strips of different widths and glue to the bag with PVA glue, smoothing down carefully to get rid of any air bubbles. Overlap the strips on the gusset and glue down. The gusset can be neatened by adding additional paper strips as desired. Create a focal point on the bag front by gluing a motif cut from patterned paper over the torn strips. I chose a dove.

TIP
Make sure all of the paper pieces are glued flat to the bag blank with no wrinkles and allow the PVA glue to dry completely before decorating further.

3 Ink up the snowflake rubber stamp with gold pigment ink and press onto the bag front, supporting the surface from underneath with your other hand. While the ink is still wet, sprinkle with a gold pearlescent embossing powder. Tap off the excess powder and gently warm with a heat gun to melt the powder onto the stamped design. Add more stamped images in this way using different sized designs for extra interest.

4 Take the blue gelly glaze gel pen and begin making a swirly pattern on the front of the bag using a series of small dots that will dry as slightly raised, shiny spots. Keep adding flourishes to fill areas that look empty. Use the gold pen to add bigger dots in the centre of the swirls or to run lines of dots parallel to the stripes on the torn paper strips.

5 While the ink is drying, make the handles. Cut two pieces of wire 35cm (13¾in) long. Bend the wire over 5cm (2in) from the end to stop the beads falling off as you thread them on. Thread on crystal, metallic and pearlescent beads in a random order until the beaded length measures 25cm (9⅞in) and bend over the remaining wire as before. Repeat with the second piece of wire. Gently curve the beaded wires into handle shapes.

TIP
DIY bag blanks can be made from a double thickness of thin card. Use a strong clear glue to hold the front and back to the gusset. Once covered, the joins will become stronger where the paper overlaps.

6 Punch holes on both sides of the bag at equal distances from the centre. Thread one end of a beaded wire through the front of one of the holes, bringing the wire up and wrapping it around the handle to lock it in place. For a decorative finish use round-nosed pliers to bend the remaining wire length into a spiral and press it flat against the surface of the bag. Repeat for the other three wire ends and reshape the handles so that they are symmetrical.

Advent Calendar

So often these days the shop-bought advent calendar is little more than a daily chocolate dispenser. Change all that by creating your own countdown calendar and filling it with a mix of little treats, from tiny toys and candies to secret festive messages. If made from a heavyweight paper or thin card, the calendar will survive being packed away ready to be brought out again next year. I've chosen to make mine in fresh pinks and greens.

This is the perfect project for using up all of your paper scraps as each pocket measures just 5 × 10cm (2 × 4in). The pockets are quick to decorate with a variety of Christmas border and motif peel-offs, and numbers of course!

POCKET TREATS
Individually decorated paper pockets are filled with tiny treats to help build up the excitement and the anticipation of Christmas day itself.

You will need

❄ Several sheets of plain and patterned 30 × 30cm (12 × 12in) heavyweight scrapbooking paper

❄ One sheet 30 × 30 cm (12 × 12in) thin card to coordinate

❄ 30 × 30cm (12 × 12in) chipboard

❄ 30 × 30cm (12 × 12in) thin card, plain

❄ Small pieces of heavyweight patterned paper in coordinating colours

❄ Narrow-tipped gold leafing pen

❄ Gold inkpad

❄ 2.5 × 1.25cm (1 × ½in) piece of wood

❄ Metallic gel pens

❄ Embellishments: selection of small gold peel-offs, including Christmas borders and motifs, circles, stars, numbers 1–24; gemstones of various sizes

❄ One sheet A4 sheet (US letter) thin gold mirror card

❄ 12mm (½in) diameter circle paper punch

❄ 15mm (⅝in) diameter star paper punch

❄ Scraps of parchment paper

❄ Thin satin ribbon

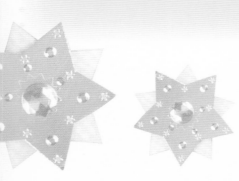

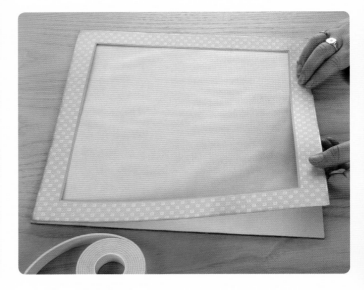

1 Cut a 2.5cm (1in) wide frame from a sheet of 30 × 30cm (12 × 12in) patterned scrapbooking paper and stick onto a coordinating square of thin card. Use a ruler and craft knife to cut the centre from the card leaving a 2mm (³/₃₂in) border inside the frame. Press the gold inkpad against the outer edges of the frame to create a slight shadow. Cover the chipboard with a contrasting sheet of plain scrapbooking paper, making sure it is stuck down well, and use the gold inkpad to colour the edges. Fix the frame to the decorated chipboard using 3D foam tape to add depth; ensure the edges are lined up accurately, as shown above.

2 Choose four coordinating sheets of heavyweight scrapbooking paper. Use the templates on pages 122 and 123 to cut out the tree branch layers from the paper, cutting sections 2 and 4 from the same paper design. Take a sheet of plain thin card and assemble the pieces of the tree on top of this. Make sure that the bottom of the smallest piece fits neatly into the top of the next like a jigsaw. Use sharp scissors to cut closely around the pieced tree design so that none of the backing sheet shows.

3 Use the gold leafing pen to trace around the lower edges of the branch layers. This will cover any gaps that may have appeared when assembling the pieces. Run the pen around the outside edges of the tree. Use a cotton bud which has been run through the gold inkpad to create a shadowed effect around the tree.

TIP
This is an ideal project to use up paper scraps. You can make your paper selection as varied as possible, using spots and stripes as well as pictorial designs.

4 Use the pocket template on page 122 to make 24 pockets from small pieces of heavyweight scrapbooking paper, each measuring 5 x 10cm (2 x 4in). Fold along the dotted score lines and use a craft knife to carefully cut the lines as marked on the template.

TIP
To make a former from chipboard, stack several 2.5cm (1in) wide strips until a 1.25cm (½in) thickness is measured.

5 To assemble the pockets, use the small piece of wood as a former to fold the paper around. This ensures that all score lines are at right angles so that each pocket will fold up neatly.

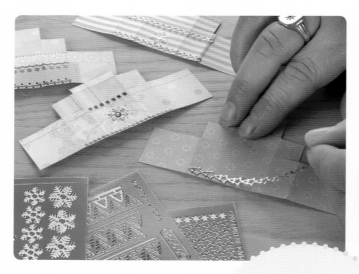

6 Flatten out the folded pockets and add a peel-off border to the centre and side panels of each. Use small peel-off motifs to decorate the centre of each pocket and add dots of metallic gel pen and tiny gemstones to finish.

TIP
Make each pocket different from the others and use the patterns on the papers to guide you when placing the borders.

7 Use the round paper punch to cut 24 small circles from leftover patterned paper. Punch 24 stars from the gold mirror card. Glue a circle to the centre of each star and use a gel pen to add a border of tiny dots around each one. Place peel-off numbers from 1 to 24 in the centre of the circles.

8 Position the tree in the centre of the frame so that the branches overlap equally on either side. Fix in place with sufficient 3D foam pads to hold the shape slightly above the frame. Lightly mark pencil crosses on the tree to indicate where each pocket will sit, using the picture on page 67 as a guide to positioning.

TIP
You can choose to either place the pockets randomly around the tree or start with the number 1 at the bottom left and work your way up to 24 at the top right.

9 Re-fold each paper pocket around the wood former and secure with double-sided tape. Fix the pockets to the tree in the marked positions, securing in place with double-sided tape and making sure that the base of the pockets sit parallel to the base of the backing board. Use the numbered stars to label each pocket, fixing them in place with 3D foam pads.

10 Cut a five-pointed star from gold mirror card and another from patterned paper. Ink the edges with the gold inkpad as before. Layer the gold star on top of the paper one so that the points alternate to create a ten-pointed shape. Decorate the outline of the star with tiny peel-off stars and gemstones, and position at the top of the tree with 3D foam pads. Fill each pocket with a tiny gift, chocolate coins or a Christmas message. Write your message on small pieces of parchment paper, roll up around a cocktail stick, and tie with thin satin ribbon.

Baby's Christmas Album

Making a personal keepsake album as a gift is a wonderful way
to show someone how special they are to you. The revolving front
panel on this mini album allows two different sides to be shown
when the book is left out on display. The method is very simple
and will work with most symmetrical shapes so that the cover
can be adapted to suit a particular occasion.

The album is held together using a wire-o binding system and
additional pages can be added easily. It's a pleasure to fill the book
with memorable photographs and captions, but if you find that
you're short of either time or pictures you can opt to leave
the pages blank.

DO A DOUBLETAKE

When you're spoilt for choice, choose
two photos and put one on either side
of the revolving panel for a keepsake
cover that's twice as nice.

You will need

❋ 30 x 30cm (12 x 12in) cardstock
  – one sheet pale blue, one sheet
  lilac, three sheets white

❋ Small pieces of coordinating card

❋ Embellishments: blue gauze ribbon;
  coloured metal gems; blue and
  gold metallic gel pens; gold leaf
  pen; star-shaped punch

❋ Photographs of your choosing

❋ 0.5mm thick wire

❋ Bind-It-All machine and white
  1.25cm (½in) binding strip

1 Cut four 15cm (6in) squares of pale blue, and four more
  from lilac cardstock. Glue together in matching pairs to
create four thicker squares. Take one blue square and fix a
25cm (10in) length of ribbon to one edge with double-sided
tape. Glue a lilac square on top, covering the end of the ribbon
and creating a heavyweight back cover for the book.

2 Take one of the remaining thick squares of card and
  draw a line down the middle. Place the large star template
(page 125) centrally on this line, slightly nearer the top of the
cover and draw around it. Use a sharp craft knife and ruler to
cut the shape out and put the resulting motif to one side. Place
the cover over the last thick square of card so that all of the
edges line up and trace around the inside of the star shaped
aperture. Cut this shape out and put to one side.

3 Take the two star cut outs and trim 1mm (¹⁄₃₂in) from the
  edges of each. Check that they are identical in size, score a
line down the centre of one star and place two strips of double-
sided tape either side of this mark to leave a 1mm (¹⁄₃₂in) groove.
Fix the other star over the top and push a 20cm (8in) length of
wire up and down the resulting channel. Remove the wire,
straighten if necessary and put to one side.

4 Place the two apertured covers together and check that all of the sides and edges line up. Trim any adjustments if necessary and score down the centre of one, making sure that the line goes through the top point and bottom indent of the star. Place double-sided tape either side of the groove as before and attach another length of ribbon to the right hand edge of the cover. Fix the covers together, enclosing the ribbon ends.

5 Put the star cut out in the aperture and run the piece of wire through the channels to hold the two components together. Check that the star will spin in its hole without catching before trimming the ends of the wire flush with the top and bottom of the cover. Squeeze a little strong clear glue into the holes on the edges of the cover and wipe away any excess before it is allowed to dry.

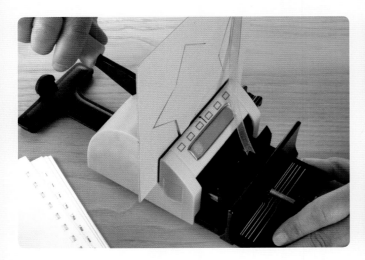

6 Mark the centre of the edge that is to be bound on both covers. The ribbons should be on the opposite edges. Use the binding machine to punch holes in each cover, starting in the middle to ensure that there is the same distance from the holes at the top and bottom corners. Cut several 15cm (6in) squares of white card and punch holes in one edge of each of these to line up with the covers.

7 Assemble the book in order, then bring the back cover around to sit on top of the front. Fit a white, wire binding strip into the holes and place in the press of the binding machine, holding the covers and pages perpendicular to the base. Squeeze the wire binding shut with the press and remove the book. Move the back cover around to the end of the book and this action will enclose the cut ends of the binding strip and neaten the whole look of the album.

8 Cut several 8cm (3⅛in) lengths of blue ribbon and trim the ends into an inverted 'V'. Fix one or two of these to each loop of the binding wire, tying securely in place. Cut a longer length of ribbon and knot this onto the top loop leaving two long ends. Cut two stars from several thicknesses of card glued together to imitate chipboard, punch a small hole in the top point of each and thread the ribbon through. Tie in a neat bow and use a little clear glue to secure the stars to the ribbon. Add decoration with smaller layered motifs, gemstones and gel pens.

9 Use a smaller version of the star template (page 125) to cut a shape from white card and matt onto a mid blue star leaving a 1mm (1/32in) border. Glue this to the centre of one side of the revolving panel. Gild the edges of a small lilac star with a gold leaf pen before matting onto blue card with a 5mm (3/16in) border and gluing to the other side. These panels will form the backgrounds for your important cover photographs that can be trimmed and matted to an appropriate size and shape.

10 Make several smaller stars from white, lilac and mid blue card, cutting the centres out of some to create shaped frames. Glue these randomly on the cover, trimming away any points that might overlap the aperture and restrict the movement of the spinning star. Decorate the outlines of the motifs with dots using metallic gel pens and glue metal gems to the centres. Punch out small stars from the remaining scraps of card to fill any empty areas of the cover.

TIP
Cut frames, motifs and caption panels from coordinating card. These can be wrapped in cellophane and presented with the album as a do it yourself gift, along with a stock of photos and double-sided tape.

SURPRISE PHOTO CARD

You will need

❋ Large pink card blank
❋ Red, green and pink card
❋ Coloured insert
❋ Ribbon
❋ Red diamanté and gold star gems
❋ Star punch

This flip around greeting allows you to show off your expert card-making skills. The technique works in the same way as the album but is faster, as it uses a length of twisted ribbon instead of wire to hold the swinging disc in the centre.

1 Cut a square aperture from the front of the card blank and cut two circles of red card to easily fit into this square. Glue the circles together, sandwiching a length of narrow ribbon between them. Mount a photo on one side and decorate the other, as shown above.

2 Open the card blank and position the circle in the centre of the aperture. Fix the ribbon to the bottom of the frame with double-sided tape. Twist the ribbon at the top once, secure in the same way, and trim both of the ends to the edges of the card. Cut another square aperture frame to match the card and glue over the top to hide the ribbon ends. A narrow light green aperture border can be added to the front of the card for extra interest.

3 Fix a coloured insert to the fold of the card with narrow double-sided tape. This will act as a background to your decoration, as well as giving you somewhere to write your greeting.

Crown Box Trio

The story of the three wise Kings inspired me to create this gift box trio. Each box looks like a miniature crown intricately decorated with cut out patterns in luxurious gold and silver, and sumptuous jewel colours. Pack with homemade goodies such as coconut ice wrapped in white tissue paper or piles of Christmas cookies. Alternatively, make miniature versions and add a hanging ribbon for stunning tree decorations.

The simple curved folding pattern at the top of the box produces a stunning decorative lid, and the secret to success is the careful measuring and scoring of the fold lines. A medium-sized box is shown being made in the step instructions overleaf.

A CUT ABOVE

Decorate the box sides with embellished cut out patterns. Templates for three decorative designs have been provided on page 124. Simply reduce or enlarge these to fit the width of the box panels.

You will need

❊ Two sheets A4 (US letter) brightly coloured textured card

❊ Small, ball-ended embossing tool

❊ Gold inkpad

❊ Small pieces of metallic gold card

❊ Embellishments: satin ribbons, varying widths; small sequins in coordinating colours; gelly roll and opaque gel pens in jewel colours; multi surface metallic liner pen

1 Take one sheet of A4 (US letter) card and score across its short width at 5.8cm (2⅜in) intervals to make the box's five side panels and a 1cm (⅜in) wide end flap. To make the top folds of the box, score a line down the length of the card 4.8cm (1⅞in) from one edge, intersecting the side panel score lines. Measure 9cm (3½in) from this line and score another line to create the box's height. Leave an additional 2cm (¾in) strip of card below this to make the tabs to stick the base of the box on, and then cut off the remaining card.

TIP
You can vary the height of the box according to gift size. Just remember to leave at least 2cm (¾in) between the score line and the edge of the card to make the tabs to stick the base of the box on.

2 Mark the midpoint of each side panel at the top edge of the box. Find a plate or glass dish with a suitable diameter that will allow you to trace a gentle curve from one of these points down to the intersection of the score lines. Holding the utensil in place, score around the arc with a small, ball-ended embossing tool. Move the utensil around and score curves from either side of the midpoints down to the intersection, making ten curves in total.

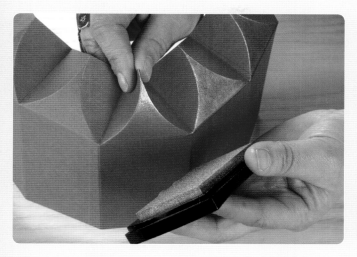

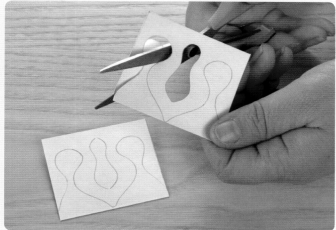

3   Gently fold the curves with pressure from your fingertips. It may help to flip the card over and re-score the straight lines of the lid section, as they will need to fold in the opposite direction to the curves and the rest of the box. Once you have defined the curved folds, colour the semi-triangular sections created by dabbing a gold inkpad over the surface and leave to dry completely.

4   Check that the distance between each side panel score line is 5.8cm (2¼in) and cut five pieces of metallic gold card 5.8 × 5.3cm (2¼ × 2¹⁄₁₆in). Use the template on page 125 to trace the side panel pattern onto the reverse of the gold card pieces and cut out with scissors or a craft knife.

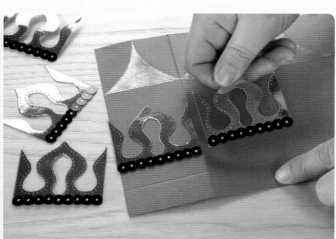

5   Use very narrow double-sided tape to fix a line of small sequins along the bottom edge of the cut out patterns. Fill in the sequin holes with dots of multi surface metallic liner pen to hide the tape. Use the gelly roll opaque gel pens to draw a symmetrical pattern of dots onto the shiny surface of the cut out patterns, and leave to dry completely.

6   Glue the cut out patterns onto each side of the box about 1cm (³⁄₈in) up from the base line. Make sure that the sides of each pattern piece butt up to the next exactly on the score line and trim down slightly if necessary. Take care to keep the pattern pieces parallel to the card base line so that when the box is glued together the first and last panels align perfectly.

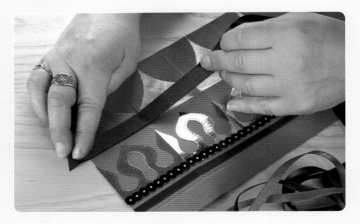

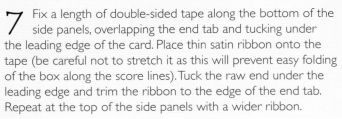

7 Fix a length of double-sided tape along the bottom of the side panels, overlapping the end tab and tucking under the leading edge of the card. Place thin satin ribbon onto the tape (be careful not to stretch it as this will prevent easy folding of the box along the score lines). Tuck the raw end under the leading edge and trim the ribbon to the edge of the end tab. Repeat at the top of the side panels with a wider ribbon.

8 Snip into the score lines at the base of the box up as far as the intersections. Trim into the end flap to make two separate tabs with tapered sides. Join the sides of the box and lid section together with double-sided tape, making sure the ribbon ends are neatly tucked out of sight. Bend the base tabs in and hold together lightly with more tape so that the box forms a pentagon shape. You may need to manipulate the sides to ensure the box is not lopsided before fixing the base tabs.

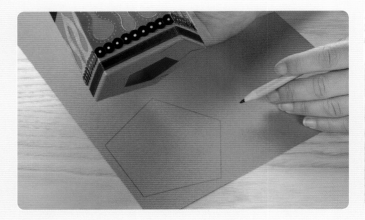

9 Place the box onto a piece of card and carefully draw around the base. Cut out the pentagon approximately 2mm (³⁄₃₂ in) inside the drawn line and check that it fits the bottom of the box tidily. If it does not appear to fit at all, check that it's at the correct orientation as you may have inadvertently twisted it around or turned it over while cutting it out. Place the box over the top of a tin can or similar flattish surface and apply double-sided tape to the base tabs. Press the base firmly in position.

10 Gently fold in the top of the box so that the points of each section meet. If the lid does not stay closed, snip a small triangle off each point and push the lid closed again. Continue snipping tiny amounts off each of the five points until a perfect fit is achieved so that the box lid looks slightly cushioned and is not completely flat.

TIP
It is easy to adapt both the five-sided and six-sided box (shown opposite) to fit the size of the gift, and useful diagrams are provided on pages 124–125 to assist with this.

LITTLE OR LARGE?

You will need

* One sheet A4 (US letter) blue card
* One sheet A4 (US letter) cream hammered card
* Small pieces textured pearlescent card, light blue mid blue, cream and pink
* Embellishments: white and pink inkpads; white and blue gelly roll pens; ribbons; gemstones; snowflake punch

Custom-made boxes are a great way to present almost any gift, from perfume to homemade preserves. The basic box instructions are very adaptable and a six-sided version is just as easy to make. Subtle pastel shades have been used with simple cut out shapes that look particularly effective when matted onto a slightly darker shade of card.

1 Each box is made following the main project instructions, but adapting the measurements according to the gift size. Use the diagrams on pages 124–125 as a guide.

2 The background of the blue box is decorated with a dotted pattern and gemstones scattered between the matted card stars. Thin strips of ribbon are added to the top and bottom edges. The box lid has been sponged with an opaque white inkpad and edged with dots of blue glossy gelly roll pen.

3 For the pink box, a bright pink inkpad has been pressed against the folds of the assembled box to give a semi-distressed feel. This has been teamed with wide bands of satin ribbon overlaid with dark pink gauze. Punched snowflake motifs decorate the cut out shapes and pale pink sparkly gemstones have been glued into the centre of each snowflake. A coordinating tag has been made to hang from the box lid, which has been topped off with gauze and satin ribbons.

DECORATING

There is no better time than Christmas to make all sorts of paper accents to brighten up your home, from shimmering tree decorations to stunning table centrepieces. Here are five great projects to get you started.

The colourful strings of the **Folk Art Bunting** can double up as a Christmas card holder and the spinning **Hanging Tree Decoration** will look great hanging at the window or on the tree. **The Sleigh Sweet Dish** will help you to keep up a regular flow of treats throughout the festivities, while the **Christmas Wreath** offers a bright welcome for guests visiting your home. The **Cascading Lantern** is the ideal finishing touch to the perfectly-laid Christmas table.

For a coordinated look, you can make all of the decorations using the same colour scheme, or mix and match as you choose.

Folk Art Bunting

Plain rooms and hallways can be given a festive treat by stringing lengths of colourful bunting along the walls. If you're short of time, plain pennants in bright colours or beautiful metallics will look stunning en masse, but if you fancy exercising your creative talents there's plenty of scope to let your imagination run wild, as seen here. Adding mini pegs between the bunting will allow you to display greeting cards in addition to your decorations.

For a wonderful three-dimensional effect, hang your bunting across the middle of a room or hallway, but don't forget that the back should look as pretty as the front. It's easier to decorate both sides of the triangles with pens before going wild with your 3D elements.

A STITCH IN NO TIME!

For a fantastic rustic look without the sewing, gel pens are perfect for adding small stitch marks without losing the textured effect.

You will need

❋ Plain and textured coloured card, assorted colours

❋ Glaze, metallic and opaque gel pens, assorted colours

❋ Chalk inkpads

❋ Embellishments: raffia; narrow ribbon; jingle bells; mini coloured pegs; 0.5mm thick copper wire

❋ Round-nosed pliers

❋ Strong cotton cord

1 Using the pennant template (page 126), cut several triangles from different coloured plain and texured card. Alternatively, cut a strip of card 12cm (4¾in) wide and mark along each side at 4cm (1½in) intervals. Join up the alternate marks on one side with the diagonally opposite mark on the other to make a series of zigzags that will cut up into equal triangles. Decorate each pennant in a different way, using the photographs of the finished bunting as a guide.

2 Try cutting a smaller triangle out of the centre of some of the pennants. The remaining pennant frame can be embellished with a decorative shape (see step 3). Glue the cut triangle to the centre of another coloured triangle. Continue to create frames and borders for the pennants in this way. For decorative detail try adding fake stitching with gel pens or run a gilding pen along the card edges to give a subtle gold border. Punch two small holes in the top of each pennant.

3 Use the motif templates (page 126) to cut a variety of decorative shapes from scrap pieces of card in the same colours as the triangles. Add decoration to these motifs with gel pens, chalks, raffia bows and bells. Fix the decorated motifs to the middle of each pennant, making sure that the colours contrast. Use 3D foam pads to lift the centrepieces away from the background.

4 To make the wire-sprung embellishments, cut more medium-sized hearts and stars from card and add decorative detailing to these on both sides with the gel pens. Add smaller motifs to their centres with 3D foam pads, or glue on ribbon bows. Punch a small hole at the top of each.

TIP
Always cut more triangles and motifs than you think you need. They won't go to waste and you can snuggle up on the sofa for a few hours to decorate them before assembly!

5 Wind a 10cm (4in) length of copper wire around a pen to make a coil and stretch out slightly. Use round-nosed pliers to bend the ends of the wire into rings and fix one loop into the hole in the embellishment.

6 Cut a length of strong cotton cord, at least ten per cent longer than required to allow for knotting. Work from the middle of the cord out in both directions to avoid it getting too tangled and knot the cord into each hole in the pennants. Intersperse the triangles with the coiled wire charms and add small coloured pegs in some places to clip cards or other motifs in place.

TIP
It is fun to make your own pennant decorations, but if time is short raid your papercraft supplies to find suitable embellishments. As you can see, I have used the occasional ready-made item myself.

TRIANGLE CARDS

Turn the pennants around and you have the beginnings of unique Christmas cards. Alternatively, made in a variety of sizes, the upside-down pennant cards can be displayed on a windowsill or bookshelf in place of the usual candles or foliage.

You will need

* Plain and textured coloured card, assorted colours
* Glaze, metallic and opaque gel pens, assorted colours
* Chalk inkpads

1 Use the pennant template (page 126) to cut the card shape by simply laying one long edge of the template against the fold of a card blank, so that the top point sits at the top of the card. Trace around the remaining sides and cut out.

2 To make a larger triangle extend the long lines and ensure that the base is cut parallel to the original short edge.

3 Use the card blank leftovers and additional card scraps and embellishments to decorate the card fronts. Follow the decoration ideas shown here and on the bunting.

Sleigh Sweet Dish

How many times have you bought a huge tin of mixed chocolate sweets only to find that the children eat all of the good ones leaving behind the least favourites? Avoid this by making lots of little dishes to scatter around the house at Christmas and dole out treats on a daily basis to ensure that everyone gets their fair share.

The main body of the sleigh is cut from one sheet of card. The addition of runners, cut from double thickness card and set at a slight angle, support this sturdy dish. The sleigh can be decorated in a number of ways and the intricate cutwork patterns cut into the glitter card side panels are particularly eye-catching.

DECORATIVE DETAILING
The cutwork panels are further enhanced with the addition of dots of opaque gel pen that follow the swirling lines of the design.

You will need

❋ Two sheets A4 (US letter) medium-weight card, deep pink
❋ One sheet A4 (US letter) green glitter card
❋ White opaque gel pen

1 Use the large sleigh body template (page 121) to cut the sleigh from the deep pink card. Score the lines around the base rectangle and along each side tab. Fold along all of the score lines and sharpen the creases with a bone folder. Fix double-sided tape to each side tab and join the side panels to the front and back pieces so that the tabs sit on the inside of the sleigh.

2 Trace the large sleigh decorative side panel designs (page 120) onto the back of the glitter card. Ensure that you mirror the pattern for the two side panels. Alternatively, create your own design but use the panels of the sleigh body template as a guide to how large the patterns need to be. The front and back sections should be exactly the same width as the template, but the side panels can overlap to form decorative features. Cut out the design with a sharp craft knife starting with the interior of the pattern and cutting the outline last.

TIP
When cutting out an intricate design with a craft knife it is easier to rotate the card than the knife, especially on tight curves. For more advice, see page 18.

TIP
To make a simpler dish without runners, use the small sleigh templates on pages 120 and 121. Gold card has been used for the base and white card for the decorative panels.

3 Place the glitter card up against the sleigh sides to check the fit and trim if necessary. Make a pencil mark where the cut outs overlap the sleigh and colour those areas on the wrong side of the glitter card with metallic pen to coordinate with the base colour. Use a glue stick to coat the cut out panels and fix to the sleigh, ensuring that the bottom edges line up neatly.

4 Glue two pieces of medium-weight card together to make a thick sheet. Use the template on page 121 to cut out the runners from the thick sheet of card. Score where the legs of the runners meet the sleigh base. Fold along the score lines and flatten the card again. Use the white opaque gel pen to decorate the top side of the runners with a series of linked spirals and leave to dry.

5 Cut a piece of card 1.5 × 6.5cm (⅝ × 2½in) and score 1cm (⅜in) in from each end. Use double-sided tape to fix one folded end of the card strip to the centre of one runner. Stick the other end of the strip to the other runner to make the runner legs splay out slightly to provide a firm support for the sleigh.

6 Place the runner on the base of the sleigh with the longer curved parts at the front. Fix double-sided tape to the front and back of the base of the runners and fix in place.

PRETTY PLACE SETTINGS

Why not try an alternative to crackers this year – use the sleigh base to make trinket trays laden with goodies to decorate table place settings. Fill the trays with tiny wrapped novelties, sweets, party poppers and handwritten jokes rolled into a scroll and tied with ribbon. Finish by placing a label on each to ensure that everyone sits in the right place.

You will need

* One sheet A4 (US letter) medium-weight card or heavyweight patterned paper
* Embellishments: grosgrain ribbon; ric-rac braid; beaded trims; buttons; embroidery thread
* Metallic pen

1 Use the small sleigh body template (page 121) to make the trinket tray following instructions in step 1, page 94.

2 Decorate the panels as you choose. Lengths of ric-rac braid can be fixed in place with double-sided tape. Metallic beaded trims make a striking edging on plain coloured card. Or wrap striped grosgrain ribbon around the sleigh, pinching at the corners and making sure that the ribbon stays parallel to the bottom of the tray.

3 If using patterned card to make the trays, add coloured buttons tied with embroidery thread and dots of metallic pen to enhance the designs.

TIP
Personalize each dish with the addition of a hand cut monogram glued to the sides. Use a contrasting glitter card to really make these stand out.

Christmas Wreath

Show off your papercrafting skills with this beautiful and luxurious Christmas wreath, which combines glitter card, sparkling beads, shimmering acetate, sumptuous ribbon and delicate cut paper shapes. This garland creates a perfect focal point for an interior door or for the mantelpiece.

To make the wreath, decorative details are layered onto a ribboned base ring. There are bead clusters in berry colours, glittery sprigs of holly and ivy, and delicately paper-sculpted doves. The good news is that the berries, leaves and birds can be made whenever you have a spare moment, and the complete wreath assembled when you have more time.

FLIGHTS OF FANCY

The two paper-sculpted doves add the perfect finishing touch to this festive wreath. To make each bird you will need to cut six pieces from pearly white card and assemble following the simple instructions provided.

You will need

❋ Thin card (recycled cereal packet is ideal)

❋ Kitchen paper

❋ Light green, dark green and red raffia

❋ 30 × 30cm (12 × 12in) sheet of
  iridescent acetate

❋ Blue and green tissue paper

❋ Cardstock: green and gold glitter; green
  textured pearlescent; pearly white

❋ Fine glitter, green and gold

❋ Metallic gel pen

❋ Copper wire

❋ Glass beads and pearls in berry colours,
  ranging from seed beads up to 6mm
  (¼in) diameter

❋ Round-nosed pliers

❋ 1m (1⅛yd) wide red ribbon for hanging

❋ Satin and gauze ribbon in greens, golds and
  reds, in a variety of widths, cut to 4–5cm
  (1½–2in) lengths

1 Cut a 23cm (9in) diameter circle from a double thickness of
thin card. Draw a 15cm (5⅝in) diameter circle in the centre
and cut out to create a ring 4cm (1½in) wide. Roll up several
sheets of kitchen paper into thin tubes and glue these around
the ring to raise the surface. Tear 5cm (2in) wide strips of
kitchen paper and wrap around the ring to hold the tubes in
place and to smooth the curve created.

2 Cut 1m (1⅛yd) lengths of red and green raffia and ease the folds out to make wide strips of creased paper. Secure the strips at the back of the ring and begin wrapping around, alternating the colours to create a striped pattern. Join lengths of raffia by knotting together at the back of the ring.

3 Cut eight 15cm (5⅞in) squares from the tissue paper and four from the the iridescent acetate. Crumple and flatten the squares. Paste one side of the acetate with slightly watered-down PVA glue. Lay a sheet of tissue paper on top and smooth down with more PVA glue. Lay a different coloured tissue-paper square on top and flatten with your hand. Leave the pasted sheets to dry before tracing around the holly leaf templates (page 125) onto the tissue side of the sheets and cutting out.

4 Take a holly leaf and crease down the centre, following the curve of the shape. Make creases from the tip of each prickle to the central spine of the leaf by pressing between your thumb and forefinger. If areas of the acetate appear to lift from the tissue paper you can re-glue them. Alternatively, you can leave them as they are to add extra dimension to the leaves.

TIP
To draw the fine lines of glue onto the holly leaves, you may find that a ballpoint glue pen gives you more control and therefore, a better result.

5 Cut approximately 30 holly and ivy leaves from the glitter and textured pearlescent card using the templates on page 125. Run fine lines of PVA glue down the centre of each holly leaf and out to each point. Quickly sprinkle fine glitter over the glue lines before they dry and shake off any excess. Use a glue pen to draw intricate veining lines on the ivy leaves and brush a small amount of PVA glue around the edges of each before adding fine glitter as before.

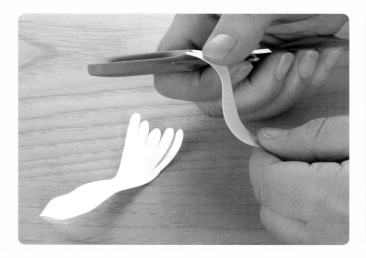

6 Trace both the dove body templates (page 125) onto the pearly white card and cut out using small sharp scissors. Carefully rub away any pencil marks and ensure that the wing tips and tail feathers are cut long enough. Curl the body pieces over the blade of a pair of scissors. Flip the body over and curl the tail feathers in the opposite direction. Layer the two body pieces together with small 3D foam pads.

7 Trace the two pairs of wings onto the pearly white card. Gently curl each piece over the blade of a pair of scissors and glue each pair together on the rounded edge. Fix the wings to the body piece, placing the shorter wing behind the dove and the longer, thinner wing at the front. Add a small eye with the metallic gel pen. Now make up a second dove facing the opposite way.

8   Cut a 20cm (8in) length of copper wire and thread a varied assortment of about eight or nine glass beads onto the wire. Twist the ends together underneath the beads to form a loop. Add more beads to each end of the wire and twist into loops to make a cluster of berries. Leave the remaining ends of wire as these will be needed to fix the cluster onto the wreath.

9   Tie a wide ribbon hanging loop to the wreath, covering any stray ends with a neat bow. Trim one end of the short ribbon lengths into an inverted 'V' to prevent fraying. Lay narrow ribbon pieces onto a strip of double-sided tape. Fix the tape to the back of the wreath opposite the hanging loop, and peel away the backing. Lay wider ribbon pieces onto the tape to overlap the first row of ribbons. Build up the ribbon layers by fixing double-sided tape over the top; secure the last layer with clear tape. Continue to make six ribbon sprays and position equally around the garland.

10   Turn the ribboned wreath over and begin layering the leaves in clusters, positioning them in the spaces between the ribbon sprays. Use a combination of holly and ivy and make sure each leaf is placed so that it appears to start at the centre of the cluster. Use 3D foam pads to hold in place and tape the loose ends of the wired berries underneath the last leaf in the cluster to hold the beads in place. Add a pair of doves to either side of the wreath with 3D foam pads.

Hanging Tree Decorations

Large dangling Christmas decorations look so impressive twisting and turning on the tree. Alternatively, fix them to suspend freely above radiators or at the window so that they move continuously in the air currents, and add plenty of glitter and sparkle to catch the light. This three-piece Christmas tree is weighted at the bottom with a glass bead tassel, but each section can turn freely.

The tree sections are made from simple card cones decorated with eyelets, brads, gemstones and glitter in toning colours. I have used pale shades of peacock colours for my colour scheme, but traditional Christmas brights would stand out beautifully against a neutral backdrop.

CONE FREE
Three card cones are stacked in decreasing size from bottom to top, and as they are held together by a bead string they are free to move independently from each other.

You will need

❄ Medium-weight patterned paper in three coordinating colours

❄ Fine glitter in a contrasting shade

❄ Embellishments: star-shaped paper punch; eyelets and eyelet setting tools; mini brads

❄ Assorted glass seed beads and pearls

❄ Cotton thread and beading needle

TIP
Use a small soft paintbrush to remove any stray glitter flecks once the glue has dried completely.

1 Use the templates on page 126 to cut the cone sections from three coordinating patterned papers. Each cone section will require two shapes to be cut from the same piece of paper at the same orientation.

2 Use a glue pen to run a line of liquid glue along the shaped edge of each piece of paper and sprinkle with the fine glitter before it dries. Shake off any excess glitter and leave to dry.

3 To make the glitter stars, stick a piece of wide double-sided tape onto scrap paper, but do not remove the backing sheet, and punch out approximately 20 stars from it. Peel away the backing sheet and push the stars, sticky side down, onto a heap of the fine glitter.

4 Arrange the stars on each cone half section and lightly glue in place. Fix eyelets to the centre of each star (see page 19).

TIP
When decorating the cone half sections, do take care to keep the side tabs free of embellishments as these will be joined to their matching half.

5 Working on the front of the cone half sections, use a craft knife to cut 3mm (⅛ in) long slits randomly between the glitter stars. Pass a mini coloured brad through each slit and turn over to splay out the arms on the back of the paper to fix (see page 19).

TIP
If the hanging decoration is to be viewed from below, glue shaped patterned paper to the wrong side of each piece before sticking together to hide the backs of the brads and eyelets.

6 Fold the side tabs of each cone half section under and sharpen the crease with your fingernail. Check that the corners of the tabs cannot be seen and trim if necessary.

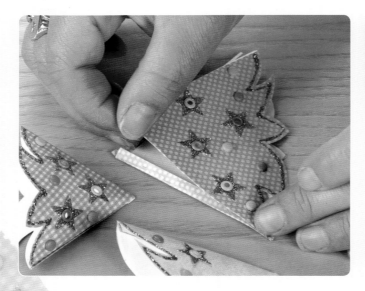

7 Fix narrow double-sided tape to the tabs on one section and join it to its matching half. Press firmly on the join before squeezing the edges towards the middle to form the section into a cone.

8 Take a 40cm (15⅝in) length of cotton and tie a knot 10cm (4in) from its end. Using a beading needle, thread several seed beads and pearls onto the thread. Skipping the last bead to be threaded on, push the needle back through all of the beads to bring the thread back to the beginning and knot the threads together. Make more chains of beads in the same way to make a tassel.

9 Knot the tassel threads to a longer piece of cotton and thread a large glass bead over the knots to hide them. Begin threading coloured seed beads onto the long thread and continue until it measures 6cm (2⅜in). Thread a large pearl onto the cotton to act as a stop and pass the needle through the slot at the point of the largest cone.

10 Thread more seed beads onto the cotton above the largest cone until it measures 4cm (1½in), add a pearl bead and pass the needle through the middle cone. Thread a further 2cm (¾in) length ending with a pearl bead and thread through the final and smallest cone. Thread on sufficient seed beads to make a hanging loop.

FUNKY FAIRY

Flattened cones make an ideal base for a number of hanging decorations that consist of adding embellishment to a main 'body' piece. This fantastic fairy is made from two narrow cone shapes, one tucked inside the other, and with deep decorative scallops cut into the edges.

You will need

* One sheet A4 (US letter) each of light pink and deep pink card
* Pink and silver metallic pens
* Crystal gemstones
* Pink gauze ribbon
* Craft wire
* Paper ball
* Metallic thread and wool off-cuts
* Scraps of silver card
* Silver inkpad

1 Using the template on page 120, cut two cone patterns each from the light pink and the deep pink card. Cut a deep decorative scallop border on the edge of each and decorate with metallic pen work and gemstones.

2 Cut the gauze ribbon into short lengths and fix to the undersides of the light pink card pieces before creating the cones and layering the two together. Bend the end of a piece of wire into a large loop and thread through the body so that the straight end sticks out of the top of the cones. Fix a small paper ball, painted as a face, onto the wire. Make

hair by gluing a wool and metallic thread tassel onto the top of the ball. Tie two pieces of the metallic thread together to make a hanging loop.

3 Add a silver card crown and thread the hanging loop through the middle of it. Cut wings from the deep pink card using the template on page 120, and sponge the edges with a silver inkpad. Draw on a symmetrical swirly design with the silver pen and add a dotted border with the pink pen. Curl the wings inwards slightly before fixing to the back of the cone with double-sided tape.

Cascading Lantern

One of the pleasures of Christmas day is the laying of the table with gleaming cutlery, pristine glassware and the best china dusted off for the occasion. Complete the setting by adding this shimmering and simple-to-make centrepiece to the prepared table.

Made in the style of a Chinese lantern, the centrepiece has an explosion of baubles emerging from its top like a fibre optic lamp, simply made from acetate strips and paper-decorated circles. Holographic and metallic card detailing will reflect candlelight or fairy lights for a truly glittering effect. Once the table is cleared, the lantern can take pride of place on the mantelpiece.

BAUBLE EXPLOSION

The acetate strips emerging from the centrepiece are sandwiched between card circles of varying sizes. The circles are arranged along the length of the strips, to create an eye-catching and dynamic table decoration.

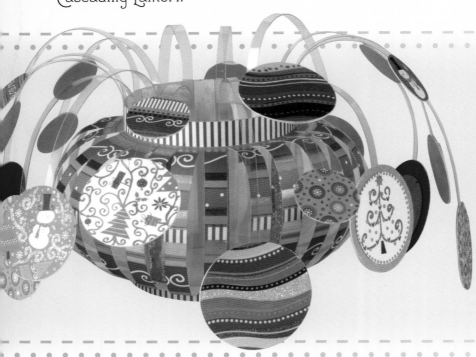

You will need

* One sheet A4 (US letter) acetate
* Pack of coordinating striped and patterned papers
* Gold metallic pen
* One sheet gold holographic card
* Circle dies and die cutter
* Small pieces of red and gold card
* Glitter

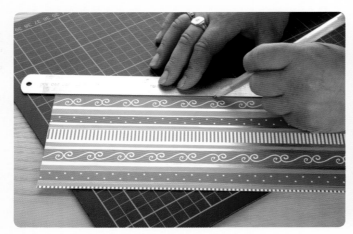

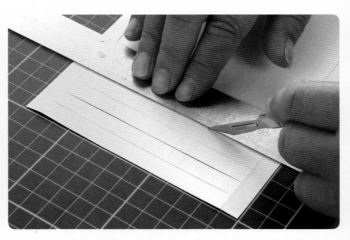

1 Cut a piece of brightly coloured striped paper 13 × 27cm (5 × 10½in) so that the stripes run parallel to the long edge of the paper. Use a ruler and a gold metallic pen to add extra stripes to the design, taking care not to smudge the ink as you move the ruler to the next position.

TIP
To avoid smudging lines of ink when moving the ruler, fix a strip of masking tape to the underside 1mm (⅟₃₂in) from the cutting edge. This is sufficient to lift the ruler away from the paper.

2 Turn the paper over and draw two lines 1cm (⅜in) in from the long edges and score. Cut across the paper at 1cm (⅜in) intervals between the two score lines. Continue cutting the whole length of the paper using the grid pattern on a cutting mat to ensure that all lines are at right angles to the long edges.

3 From the gold holographic card cut eight pieces 1 × 9cm (⅜ × 3½in) wide and glue these across a sheet cut from the acetate measuring 9 × 27cm (3½ × 10½in), starting at one short edge and leaving a 2.25cm (⅞in) gap between each to leave a blank section of acetate at the other end.

4 Stick a strip of narrow double-sided tape along one long edge of the acetate. Fold the paper rectangle along one score line and fix the folded strip to the acetate making sure the two edges line up neatly. Fold the paper back to leave the acetate uncovered and stick another strip of double-sided tape along the other edge.

5 Use a rotary cutter or craft knife and ruler to cut several long strips of acetate 5mm (³⁄₁₆in) wide. If using a craft knife and ruler, take care as the acetate is prone to slipping and you may find it helps to hold it in place on the cutting mat with masking tape.

6 Fix the acetate strips to the double-sided tape at the other edge of the acetate rectangle leaving about a 1cm (⅜in) gap between each. To keep the strips at a right angle to the edge of the acetate use the grid pattern on your cutting mat as a guide.

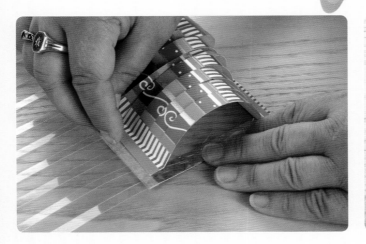

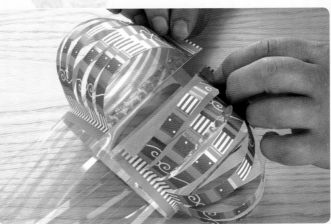

7 Fix another length of double-sided tape over the strips so that it lays directly over the first piece. Fold the patterned paper along the other score line and bring the sheet back over the acetate rectangle. Fix the two edges together so that the paper curves up in the middle and the acetate strips are secured between the two layers.

8 Cut away one strip of paper from the blank end of the acetate and stick a length of double-sided tape across the acetate in its place to join the two ends of the lantern together in a circle. Sit the lantern on its base and arrange the acetate strips so that they gently curve over the sides of the circle.

9 Die-cut several circles in different sizes from the coordinating patterned papers. Cut the same number of circles from the red, gold and holographic gold card to back the baubles. Add extra decoration to the patterned paper with metallic pens and glitter.

TIP
If you do not have a die cutter, circle punches of varying sizes could be used as an alternative to make perfect circles every time.

TIP
If you find the weight of the baubles is not enough to stop the strip of acetate from standing upright when the excess is cut away, gently crease the base of the strip where it joins the top of the lantern.

10 Spread glue over the back of a plain card circle and place behind an acetate strip. Stick a decorated paper circle, right side showing, over the top to sandwich the acetate strip. Position the circles randomly along the length of the strips, trimming away the excess acetate. Generally the smaller circles will look better closer to the lantern and the larger circles further away from it, but do vary the distances as much as possible.

TABLE DECORATIONS

The Chinese lantern technique can be used to make several different paper decorations for the Christmas table, such as a candleholder, napkin ring, wine glass charm and place card holder. Coordinating patterned papers, satin ribbons and sparkling crystal bead trims produce a matching look.

TIP

When using paper candleholders always make sure that the candle is tall enough for the flame to sit at least 5cm (2in) above the top of the decoration and never leave the burning candle unattended.

1 First, make the candleholder. Cut a small rectangle of paper from patterned paper. To make the lantern, choose a different patterned paper; cut a wider rectangle and fold in half so that the long edges meet. Lightly mark a small border line along the unfolded edge and cut slits approximately 5mm (³⁄₁₆in) apart from the marked border to the folded edge. Open and fix the long edges to those of the smaller rectangle. Curve the rectangle around and join the two short edges.

2 Make a smaller lantern in the same way to make the holder for a place card. Cut two small slits in the top of the lantern into which the decorated place card can be slotted.

3 For the napkin ring, make a paper lantern as before, but do not cut slits into the last 4cm (1½in) of the paper. Fold over the uncut section to make a flat base before joining the two ends.

4 Decorate the candleholder, napkin ring and place card holder with ribbon borders and bows. Thread the bicone crystals onto 0.6mm silver wire, twist tightly to form a stem for each bead, and glue beneath the ribbon bows to hide the ends of the wire.

5 To make the wine glass charm, wrap 1mm silver wire around a marker pen three times. Curl the ends into tight spirals with round-nosed pliers. Make a miniature lantern as before and fix to one end of the wire spiral with a loop of ribbon. To fix to a glass, wind the spiral onto its stem. Make a different coloured charm for each guest.

TEMPLATES

ACTUAL SIZE

SNOWMEN CASH CARD

ANGELIC MESSENGER

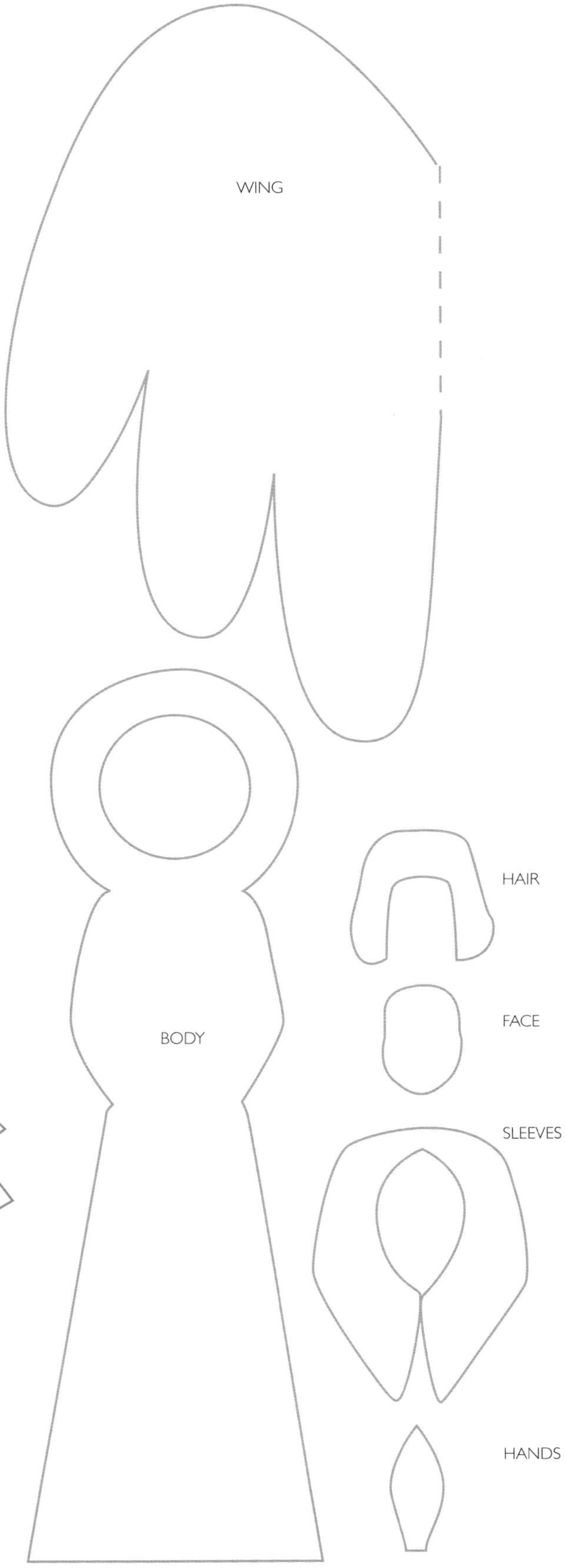

WING

RIGHT-HAND
SNOWMAN

CENTRE SNOWMAN

HAIR

BODY

FACE

SLEEVES

ARMS

LEFT-HAND
SNOWMAN

HANDS

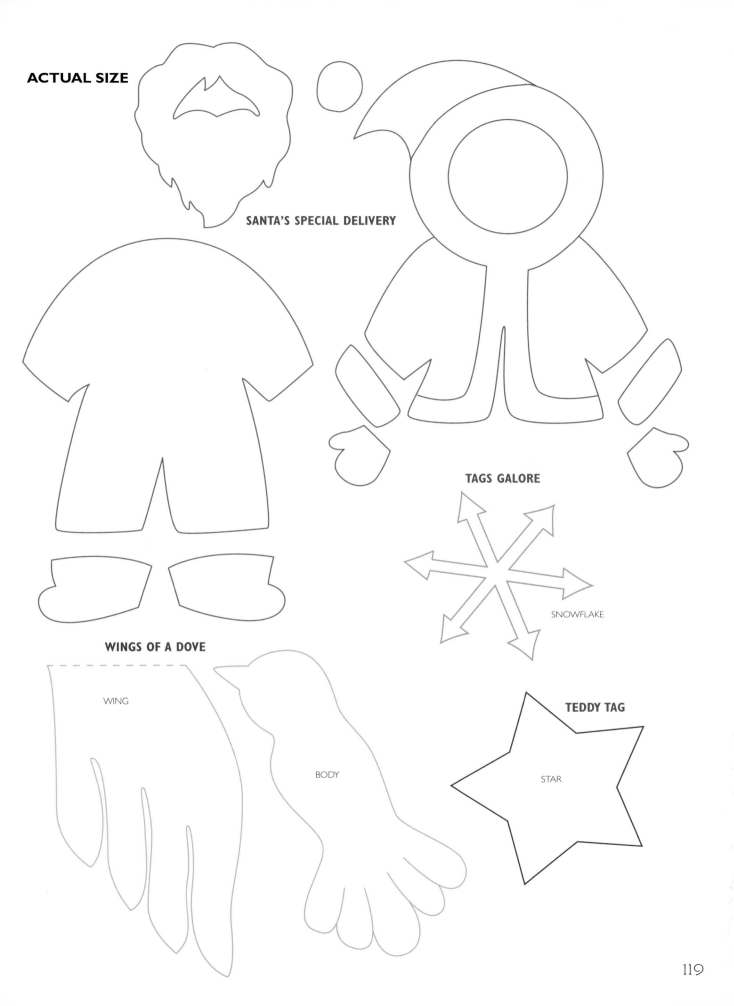

ACTUAL SIZE

SANTA'S SPECIAL DELIVERY

TAGS GALORE

SNOWFLAKE

WINGS OF A DOVE

WING

BODY

TEDDY TAG

STAR

ENLARGE BY 125%

FUNKY FAIRY

WINGS

CONE

SLEIGH SWEET DISH

SMALL SLEIGH DECORATIVE PANELS

LARGE SLEIGH DECORATIVE PANELS

SLEIGH SWEET DISH
(CONTINUED)

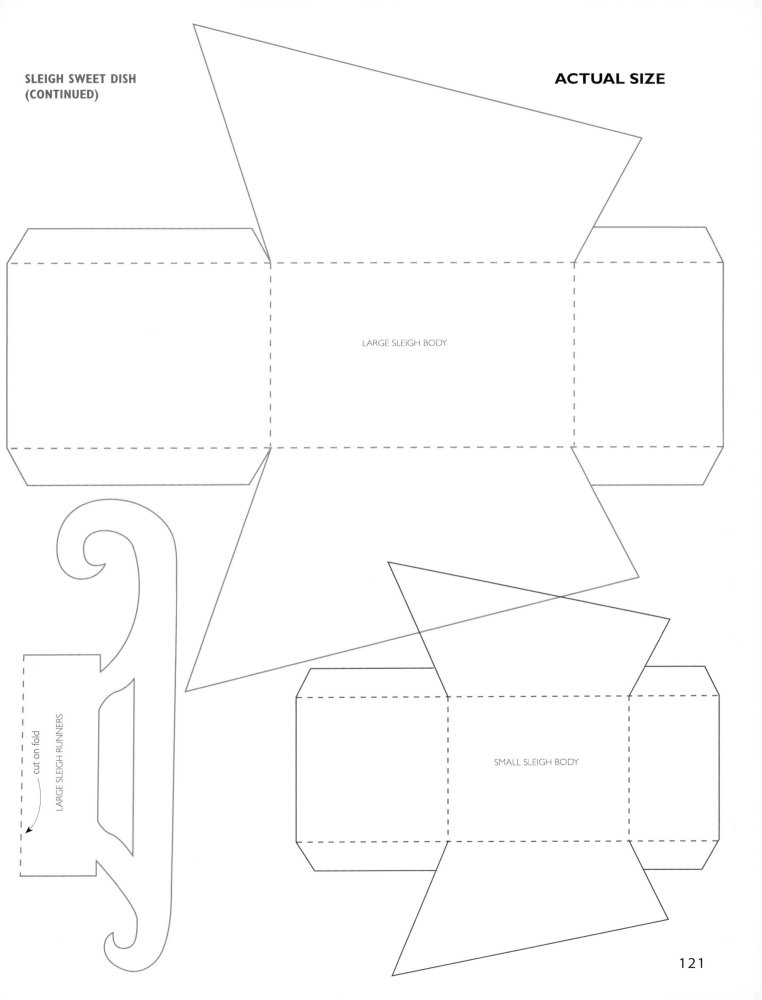

LARGE SLEIGH BODY

cut on fold

LARGE SLEIGH RUNNERS

SMALL SLEIGH BODY

ADVENT CALENDAR

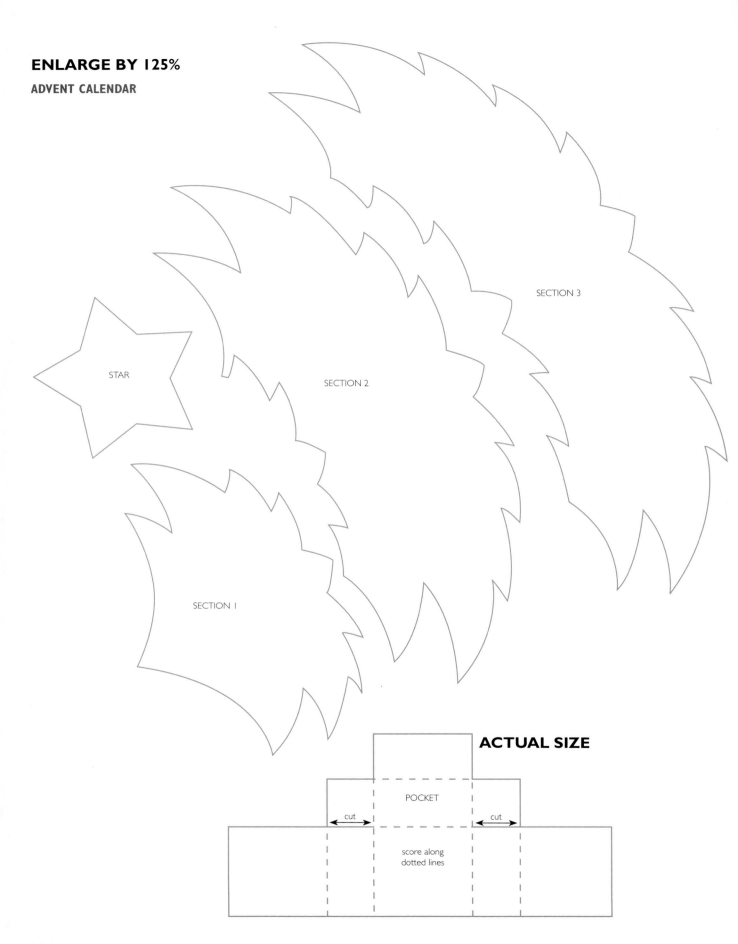

STAR

SECTION 3

SECTION 2

SECTION 1

ACTUAL SIZE

POCKET

cut

cut

score along
dotted lines

ENLARGE BY 125%

ADVENT CALENDAR (CONTINUED)

ACTUAL SIZE

HAND STITCHED STOCKING

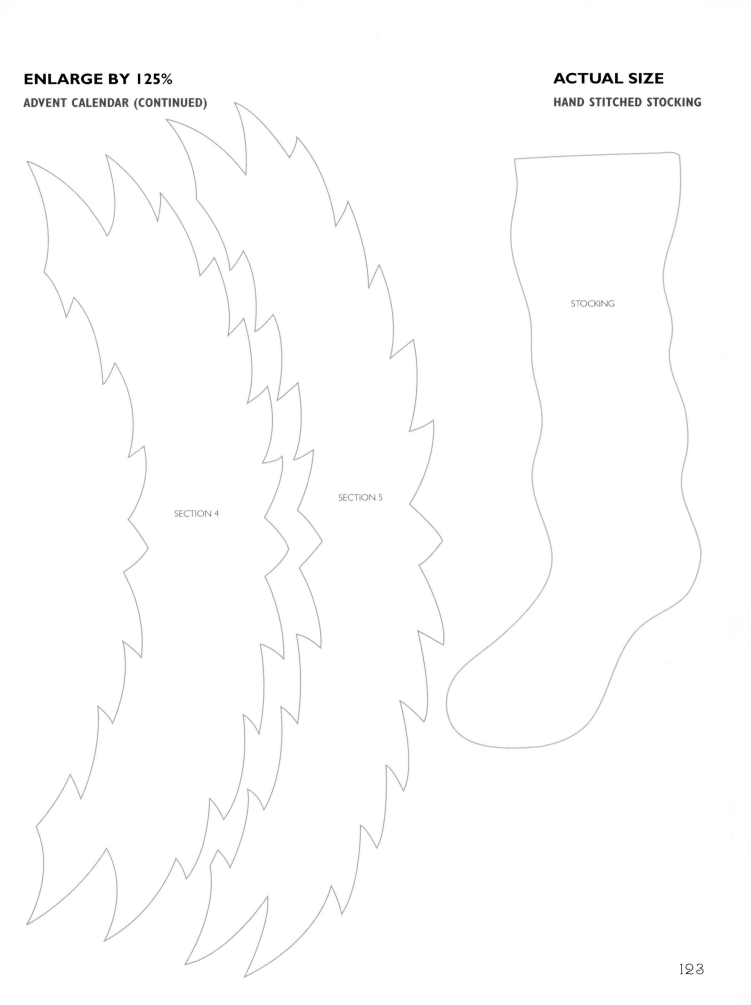

SECTION 4

SECTION 5

STOCKING

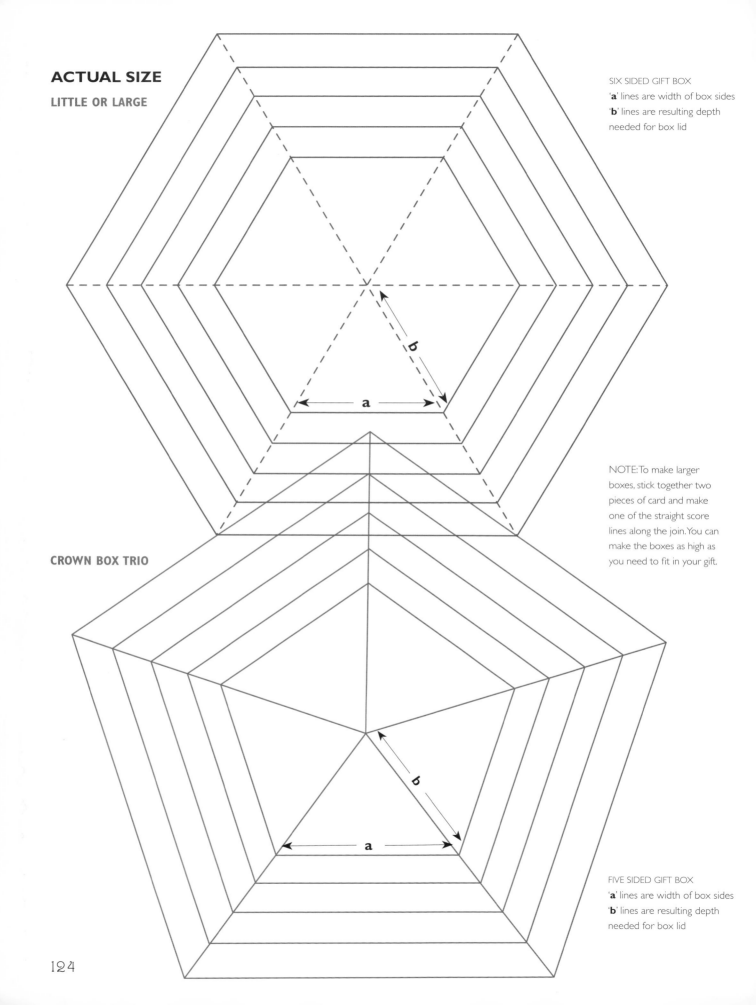

ACTUAL SIZE

LITTLE OR LARGE

SIX SIDED GIFT BOX
'**a**' lines are width of box sides
'**b**' lines are resulting depth
needed for box lid

CROWN BOX TRIO

NOTE: To make larger
boxes, stick together two
pieces of card and make
one of the straight score
lines along the join. You can
make the boxes as high as
you need to fit in your gift.

FIVE SIDED GIFT BOX
'**a**' lines are width of box sides
'**b**' lines are resulting depth
needed for box lid

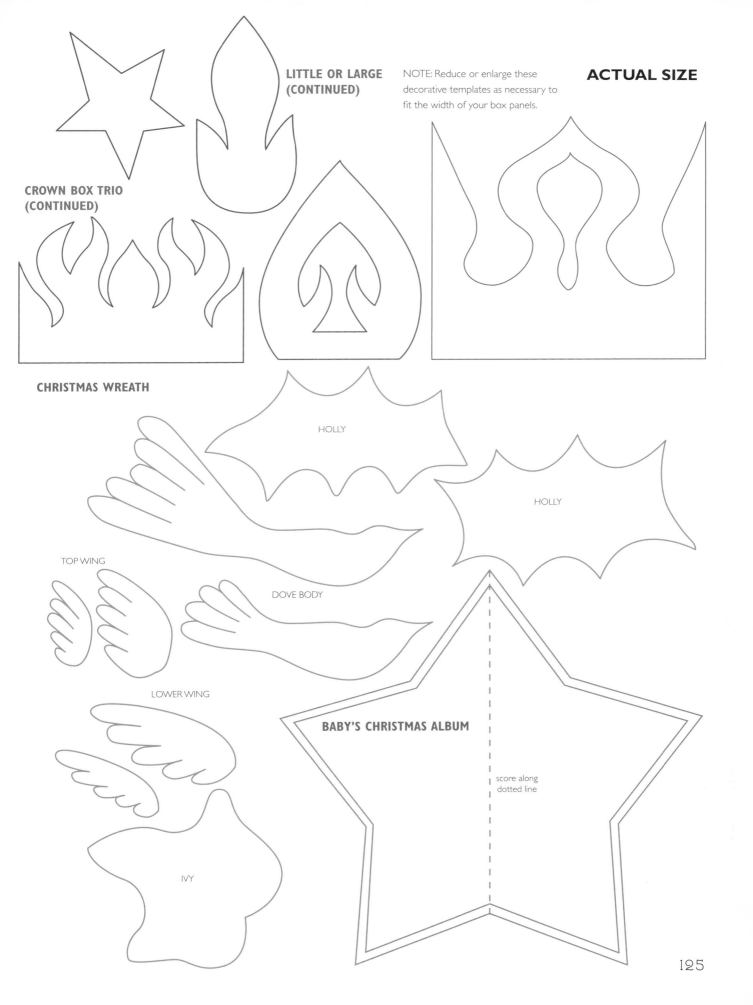

LITTLE OR LARGE (CONTINUED)

NOTE: Reduce or enlarge these decorative templates as necessary to fit the width of your box panels.

ACTUAL SIZE

CROWN BOX TRIO (CONTINUED)

CHRISTMAS WREATH

HOLLY

HOLLY

TOP WING

DOVE BODY

LOWER WING

BABY'S CHRISTMAS ALBUM

score along dotted line

IVY

ACTUAL SIZE

HANGING TREE DECORATION   **FOLK ART BUNTING**

MOTIFS

PENNANT

SUPPLIERS AND ACKNOWLEDGMENTS

SUPPLIERS

UK SUPPLIERS

The Paper Mill Shop
(branches nationwide)
www.thepapermillshop.co.uk

The Range
(branches nationwide)
www.therange.co.uk

A Card 4 U
www.acard4u.co.uk

The Stamp Man
Unit 10
Craven Nursery Park
Snaygill Ind Est
Skipton
North Yorkshire
BD23 2QR
Tel 01756 797048
www.thestampman.co.uk

Josy Rose
Tel 0845 450 1212
www.josyrose.com

Crafty Ribbons
3 Beechwood Clump Farm
Tin Pot Lane
Blandford
Dorset
DT11 7TD
Tel 01258 455889
www.craftyribbons.com

Stamposaurus Craft Supplies
3 Pocket Close
Binfield
Berkshire
RG12 8FJ
Tel 01344 481654
www.stamposaurus.co.uk

Gregory Knopp
Tel 01634 375706
www.gregory-knopp.co.uk

The Art of Craft
101 Lynchford Road
North Camp
Farnborough
Hampshire
GU14 6ET
Tel 01252 377677
www.art-of-craft.co.uk

US SUPPLIERS

Making Memories
www.makingmemories.com

Fascinating Folds
PO Box 10070
Glendale AZ85318
www.fascinating-folds.com

**Hollander's Decorative and
Handmade Papers**
410 N Fourth Avenue
Ann Arbor MI48104
Tel 734 741 7531
www.hollanders.com

Paperarts
www.paperarts.com (Arizona)

Paper Mojo
Tel 1 800 420 3818
www.papermojo.com

ABOUT THE AUTHOR

Corinne Bradd is a regular contributor to and demonstrator for specialist craft magazines, including *Crafts Beautiful*. She also designs projects for children and schools, taking advice (and polite criticism) from her young daughter, and she can regularly be seen on YouTube's 'Crafts Channel'. A self-confessed creative addict, she spends much of her free time looking for exciting and colourful materials to work with. Corinne lives in Clacton-on-Sea, Essex.

ACKNOWLEDGMENTS

I would like to thank everyone who has helped me during the writing of this book: the editorial and design team at David & Charles; everyone on the crafts team at Aceville Publications; my mum for teaching me how to make something out of virtually nothing; my dad for teaching me never to throw anything away because there will always be a use for it; and my beloved daughter, Amy, for being so patient and so proud of me.

INDEX